Living with Limoges

Debby DuBay

Schiffer Publishing Ltd ®

4880 Lower Valley Road, Atglen, PA 19310 USA

Library of Congress Cataloging-in-Publication Data

DuBay, Debby.
Living with Limoges / Debby DuBay.
p. cm.
ISBN 0-7643-1451-3
1. Limoges porcelain--Collectors and collecting--Catalogs. I. Title.
NK4399.L5 A4 2001
738.2'0944'6624075--dc21
2001003203

Designed by Bonnie M. Hensley
Cover design by Bruce M. Waters
Type set in Shelley Allegro BT/Korinna BT

ISBN: 0-7643-1451-3
Printed in China
1 2 3 4

Published by Schiffer Publishing Ltd.
4880 Lower Valley Road
Atglen, PA 19310
Phone: (610) 593-1777; Fax: (610) 593-2002
E-mail: Schifferbk@aol.com
Please visit our web site catalog at **www.schifferbooks.com**
We are always looking for people to write books on new and related subjects. If you have an idea for a book, please contact us at the above address.

This book may be purchased from the publisher.
Include $3.95 for shipping.
Please try your bookstore first.
You may write for a free catalog.

In Europe, Schiffer books are distributed by
Bushwood Books
6 Marksbury Avenue
Kew Gardens
Surrey TW9 4JF England
Phone: 44 (0) 20 8392 8585
Fax: 44 (0) 20 8392 9876
E-mail: Bushwd@aol.com
Free postage in the UK. Europe: air mail at cost.

Dedication

This book is dedicated to the following: Mary Frank Gaston, who is the leading authority and encyclopedic in her knowledge of Limoges; Nancy Lindemeyer, the Founding Editor of *Victoria Magazine* and a woman who truly empowers women in business; Oprah, the greatest single inspiration for the renewed interest in reading; and to my mom, Charlotte Klassy-DuBay, who has always inspired me to be all that I could be.

Foreword

Debby DuBay's *Living With Limoges* is itself a rarity. She is able to combine in it the experience of a long time collector, with the technical knowledge of an important dealer in the field, with the sensitivity of a personal designer. A reader could not ask for more from a writer.

The technical and historical information in *Living With Limoges* is terrific, however the unique aspect of this book is how a single piece of Limoges to a complete collection are displayed in various parts of a home. Read it—as I did—and learn.

James Gilreath

James Gilreath has been the American History Specialist at the Library of Congress. He was a fellow at the Huntington Library in San Marino, California and at Harvard University. Among his many publications are *The Judgment of Experts, Federal Copyright Records, North American Indian Portfolios, Thomas Jefferson's Library, Thomas Jefferson and the Education of a Citizen.*

Acknowledgments

Since 1975, Limoges has satisfied my spirit and helped me find that balance between my career in the United States Air Force and the world of beauty and art. I am sincerely thankful to Peter Schiffer, Schiffer Publishing Company, for providing me with this opportunity of sharing my love of Limoges and the many different ways we collectors live with our Limoges porcelain. And to my editor, Donna Baker, along with the professional Schiffer staff who are as much a part of this book as I am.

To my photographers Linda LaBonte Britt and Ann Spitaro, who I am heavily indebted to and without whose talent and professionalism this book would not have been possible.

Special recognition goes to Ellie Smerlas, President, DataStar, Inc. Waltham, Massachusetts, a talented artist who drew all of the company marks that we were unable to photograph.

To my fellow collectors, dear friends, and heroes: Trisha Coffill, Debby Lucas, Bev O'Connell, Kara Sewall, and Jim Gilreath. Their courage is inspiring. Ignoring their own special needs, they encouraged me to write a book sharing my knowledge of Limoges.

I thank the Haviland Collectors Internationale Foundation for allowing me to use the chart of Haviland marks and dates. To my colleagues: Mary Frank Gaston, Dorothy Kamm, and Faye Strumpf, whose works I have acknowledged in the Bibliography, for their professional guidance.

My friends and fellow collectors who graciously invited me into their homes and allowed to me photograph their personal pieces of Limoges: Trisha Coffill, Janet Dipple, Candy Gammal, Lisa Gronbeck, Debby Lucas, Sandy and Larry Marshall, Collette Merillat, Ellie Smerlas, Debby Streiff, and Linda Tofte.

Special thanks to Linda Berube, Yummy Mummy Cookie Factory, Andover, Massachusetts, a talented artist who is responsible for the cookie art in the photographs and to Holland's Flowers, North Andover, Massachusetts (www.hollandflowershoppes.com), who provided all of the floral designs for the book.

Special acknowledgements go to Cyndi and Lisa, Pizzano Designs, Exeter, New Hampshire. These talented artists do not see a room as four walls and a ceiling but as a canvas that can enhance a Limoges collection.

To *Victoria Magazine*, specifically Nancy Lindemeyer, Margaret Kennedy, Ann Levine, Susan George, Colleen Heather Rogan, Mary Forsell, Connie Livsey, Tara Hill, Janet Allon, and Toshi Otsuki, who provided me with opportunities that would have never been possible without their empowerment, talent, and ability to expose women in small business.

To my family: my husband, Dan Quinn, for his true love and untiring patience; my parents, Bob and Char DuBay, for providing me with a strong foundation built on love; my siblings: Lori, Mike, and David, for their technical abilities, continuous encouragement, and great ideas; all of my nieces and nephews, who I couldn't love more if they were my own: Nicole, Alisha, Thomas, Katie, Meaghan, Robert, Brendan, Bradley, MaKenzie, Erica and Alex; and my mother-in-law, Yolanda Quinn.

To the people and town of Andover, Massachusetts for their support. The opportunities the community members have provided me cannot be overlooked in the success of Limoges Antiques Shop and my confidence to write this book.

Lastly, to all of the professional men and women in the United States Air Force with whom I had the opportunity to serve. I thank each one of you very much for your contributions to my life and my book: *Living With Limoges*.

Disclaimer

The current values in this book should only be used as a guide. Pricing is a compilation of prices from current pricing guides, computer sales, auctions, and retail sales. Prices in different areas of the country vary greatly and seem to be driven by competitive collectors, decorators, or by an individual who has to have a particular piece. This book is by no means trying to set prices on pieces, but rather provides a price range for the Limoges collector.

Contents

Introduction

Limoges has the ability to inspire, and as I walk through my home I think I have arrived in Limoges heaven. Each piece of Limoges is as unique as an individual and its beauty transforms me to an era when ornate pieces of porcelain hung in gilded rooms and elegance was an everyday part of life. As a collection, their beauty is overwhelming. I want to share with you my passion for this breathtaking, three-dimensional art form. *Living With Limoges* is dedicated to hand painted Limoges porcelain and provides decorating ideas for a single piece of Limoges or for an entire collection.

As a disciplined collector, I have devoted my free time to the joy of searching for, collecting, and carefully displaying my collection of Limoges. While serving our country in the United States Air Force, I found my very first vase in 1975 in an antique shop in Paris, France. It is a large piece with flamboyant double gold handles and hand painted roses so vivid and fresh I swear I can smell their fragrance. I then became obsessed with finding the exact ormolu-mounted French cabinet with porcelain inset on the doors in which to showcase my vase—enriching the room and, more importantly, my life.

After retiring from an Air Force career, I decided to use my extensive collection of Limoges hand painted porcelain—along with a good business plan and guidance from the Small Business Administration—to turn my passion for collecting into my new profession. In 1995, I opened Limoges Antiques Shop (www.limogesantiques.com) in historic downtown Andover, Massachusetts. Entering the shop, one is overwhelmed by the diversity and beauty of Limoges porcelain. A mammoth jardinière greets visitors, dripping with gold gilt and hand painted with tulips so vibrant you swear you could pick them. The shelves are filled with vases of various shapes and sizes and a French vitrine encases tiny little bronze jewel boxes that house hundreds of hand painted brooches, buttons, and hatpins.

Collectors are educated, they are not born. And collecting Limoges as an art form should not be mistaken as a form of self-indulgence but rather embraced as another possible form of investment. (I keep telling my husband that anyway.) Everyone can afford to collect or start a collection of Limoges: plates displayed over a doorway or mirror, tea cups with or without saucers perched on a mantel, tiny hand painted buttons, or a brooch in an enchanting Limoges box are all definitions of a collection.

Room by room, this book provides the reader with ideas for displaying lovely pieces of Limoges art, providing glimpses of homes that house from one piece to entire collections of Limoges. Some pieces have found permanent residence in an apartment, a gaudy Victorian home, or a modern spacious palace.

Over the past three decades as a collector and during the last decade as a shop owner, I have met thousands of wonderful people from all over the world—decorators, art connoisseurs, dealers, and Limoges collectors—who share the appreciation and love of this beautiful art form. Once you feel the powerful passion of owning a piece of Limoges, a passion so intense that you are overwhelmed with the feeling that you just "have to have it," you have become a true collector of Limoges porcelain.

Part I

The Art of Limoges

History

Limoges! Whether the name brings to mind a region in France, the city of Limoges, or the factories that produce fine Limoges porcelain and hand painted Limoges boxes, a picture of romance, beauty, and fabulous artisans probably springs to mind.

Limoges is a French city situated about 250 miles southwest of Paris in the Vienne region. Mount Jovis rises up from the outskirts and the Vienne River meanders through the town. It was here in 1768 that kaolin (the essential ingredient of hard paste porcelain) was discovered. This discovery was monumental for France and by 1820 the city of Limoges became the major industrial center for the production of the finest hard paste porcelain in the world. Kaolin is a white clay that comes from the decomposition of granite. Kaolin, feldspar, and quartz are essential to the manufacture of hard paste porcelain, but the porcelain itself was only one of three factors that defined Limoges pieces as the finest. The other two were an abundance of the most prestigious and skilled artisans in the world and the French flair for design. These French artisans created masterpieces out of everything from decorative pieces of art to essential objects for daily use. Today, some of the most important pieces created during this era are on display at the "Musee de la porcelaine de Limoges," Limoges, France.

Hard paste porcelain was long admired by the Europeans, who were envious of the Chinese and their knowledge of the formula for production of this exquisite translucent porcelain. In 1708 Johann Friedrich Böttger, a German chemist and guest of The King of Saxony, was ordered to produce or else. He subsequently discovered the formula for this white gold and was spared his head. Böttger, now invaluable, became the head of the Meissen factory in Meissen, Germany, where production of hard paste porcelain became the first of its kind in Europe. The formula was well guarded for another sixty years until word finally leaked as workers left the factory and took the formula for the process with them. With the formula now known, and the natural essential ingredients of kaolin and feldspar found in the surrounding Limoges region (one of comparatively few areas in the world with these deposits), production of hard paste porcelain first began at Limoges.

The firing process is what makes hard paste porcelain such an exquisite, translucent form of pottery, meaning that light is able to pass through, and also forms a glaze that cannot be penetrated. To begin with, the paste in the form of the object is fired. A glaze is then applied, followed by a second firing at which time vitreosity, meaning glassiness, is attained. Because the temperature during the firing process is so intense and the glaze and the object are of similar ingredients, they melt together and fuse. This process is why Limoges hard paste porcelain glaze cannot be penetrated and will rarely craze. If you are looking at a piece of unmarked porcelain with a crackled glaze, most likely it is not Limoges.

After the first firing of the object, known as a blank, it is in a bisque form: the glaze has not been applied and the blank has not been fired for the second time. Examples of beautiful hard paste bisque are the French statuettes and figures called Chantilly ware, featuring softly draped costumes and facial expressions molded with sensitivity. Even each tiny fingernail and dainty flower petal was delicately, yet naturally formed. After the glaze is applied, followed by a second and subsequent firings, the piece achieves that glasslike finish we are more familiar with when admiring and collecting antique decorative Limoges art and dinnerware. The fired blank may be left unpainted, or decoration can be applied over or under the glaze.

During the nineteenth century, there were about thirty-two factories and sixty-two decorating studios in the Limoges region, with the number of factories increasing to forty-eight by 1920. Limoges ultimately became a generic name and has become synonymous with the many pieces that were produced in these factories. Each factory had its own porcelain and decorating marks; many factories used several different marks over the course of their porcelain production years. Currently there are more than four hundred known marks to help identify which factory produced and decorated antique pieces of Limoges.

Each factory's distinct mark, usually green in color, was put on a piece of porcelain prior to firing; this mark is known as the underglaze factory mark, the white ware mark, or the backstamp. Usually you cannot feel this mark if you run your finger over it, as it is *under* the glaze. The problem with identifying the factory that produced a piece of Limoges comes when trying to identify a piece that was produced prior to 1891 and the mandatory requirement to mark each piece with country of origin. In addition, not all pieces in a set were marked. Being familiar with Limoges blanks is very helpful, but one must keep in mind that an unmarked piece of Limoges does not command the same price as a marked piece.

Once a piece of Limoges was ready to be decorated, the factory that produced the piece may have also decorated it or the piece may have been sent to another factory in the region to be decorated. The decorating factories each had their own mark that was placed *over* the glaze, and was thus named the decorated ware or overglaze decorating mark. This mark is usually much clearer and darker in color, often red. If you run your finger over this identification mark you can feel it, since it is on top of the glaze.

Some pieces have a third mark, the French exporter's mark, or the importer's mark, which may be hard to distinguish from the factory decorating mark since they are both over the glaze. Actually, the importer's mark is one of the easiest marks to identify, as it usually states specifically the fine department or jewelry store that imported the piece of Limoges. Familiar examples are Tiffany, Saks Fifth Avenue, and Bailey, Banks and Biddle. In 1891, the United States enacted the McKinley Tariff Law stating that all pieces of porcelain produced after 1891 must contain the name of the country of origin printed on it, making this information helpful when trying to date your piece of Limoges. On the other hand, some of the first Limoges factories had the word "France" in their underglaze marks yet were producing porcelain much earlier than 1891. The early Raymond LaPorte decorating mark, the Barny & Rigoni porcelain mark, and the Gustave Demartial porcelain mark, for example, all included the word "France" in the mark prior to 1891.

Another point of confusion relates to the "Made in" marks applied in accordance with the expanded McKinley Tariff Laws. Most items after 1914 were mandated to have the words "Made in" printed on them. This, however, is generally not the rule with Limoges: most of the factories had the word Limoges somewhere in a mark printed on the piece, and it was not until after World War II (1945) that Limoges pieces had the actual words "Made in" printed on them.

Decoration

Prior to 1872, most pieces were hand painted with enamel by artists employed by Limoges factories to sit and hand paint their blanks. Using patterns as models, Limoges blanks were painted by the artist to meet the exact specifications of the decorating factory. Many professional factory artists specialized in a particular decorative theme and their pieces have become very desirable to collectors. When the piece was completed, the artists would sign their names on the front of the piece, while the factory decorating mark would be placed over the glaze on the back of the piece. The work of many factory artists has become very desirable and sought after by serious collectors. A piece with a French factory listed artist's signature may command hundreds to thousands of dollars more than one without his signature. It is easy to identify a factory hand painted piece when it is clearly marked "hand painted" or "PEINT MAIN," which in French literally means "painted by hand." Without such notation, however, many a collector has been confused when it comes to differentiating between a piece of porcelain that is hand painted, partially hand painted, or not hand painted at all. Once you become comfortable with all variations of this art form, it is as easy as telling the difference between a print and an oil painting or watercolor on canvas or board.

After 1872, many pieces of Limoges were no longer hand painted. With the introduction of engraved transfers and full color lithographic transfers came the process known as transfer ware. This occurred when an engraved transfer, like a decal, was placed under the glaze and then fired. The process is technically called *décalcomanie*. There are also many examples of blanks that were decorated using the transfer ware process but then enhanced by a factory artist who hand painted and filled in some of the transferred decoration. Additionally, many pieces with the transfer ware decoration were embellished with hand painted gold details on the feet, handles, and edges. This form of decoration is correctly called *mixtion*.

The transfer ware and mixtion processes made the decoration more durable and were used mainly on dinnerware sets and pieces that were used in some part of the dining ritual, such as platters, serving pieces, compotes, etc. Most collectors in the United States associate Limoges with the Haviland factories and the very familiar Haviland dinnerware sets that many of us were lucky enough to inherit or have passed down in our families. I highly recommend Nora Travis's book *Haviland China* for detailed information on porcelain produced specifically from those factories. Most of the pieces from the Haviland factories have an underglaze and overglaze factory mark and are factory decorated with the transfer or mixtion process. The patterns are easily identifiable with the proper research.

If the only mark present on a decorative piece of Haviland or any other piece of Limoges is the white ware or under the glaze mark, the piece was most likely hand painted but not in a factory in France.

Of course there is always an exception, that being the majority of pieces that are marked with the "Limoges, France" mark which date before 1891. This mark is under the glaze and most examples were decorated professionally in a factory in France but do not have an over the glaze decorating or export mark. From the late nineteenth century to World War I, and then until approximately the early 1930s, about half of the undecorated Limoges porcelain produced in France was exported to the United States. Such undecorated pieces of Limoges were then decorated by American artists working for a professional American art studio or by amateur china painters painting somewhere in America.

China Painting in America

China painting was made popular during the Victorian era and many American artists studied the art of china painting in Europe. A class in porcelain art was started at Ohio State University in Columbus, Ohio and in 1913 a class began at the Cleveland School of Art. Many professional art studios sprang up in the Chicago area, including White's Art Company, Stouffer Art Studio, and the Picard Factory. Readers desiring further detail on the Picard Factory will find Alan Reed's book, *Collector's Encyclopedia of Picard China,* very informative.

The biggest influence on porcelain art in America during the early 1900s was Adelaide Robineau, who, with her husband started a magazine and then authored a book on china decoration. These publications spurred on the artists of the time interested in porcelain china painting and their interest coincided with the large shipments of blank undecorated Limoges porcelain arriving from France. Madame Robineau was a pioneer in the field of china painting. She is credited with developing the color referred to as oxblood red, developing and perfecting techniques for new and unusual glazes, and perfecting the technique of excised carving, a type of relief adding dimension. Madame Robineau won many awards in Europe and the United States and an exhibit dedicated to her research and development in the field of china painting is on permanent display at the Metropolitan Museum of Fine Art in New York City.

China painting became a passion and a daily pastime for the amateur artist. Ladies of leisure would purchase blank pieces of porcelain, not discriminating against any of the Limoges factories exporting their wares, and paint them as creatively as their imagination would allow—although flowers and fruits were the most popular. Most pieces were painted to reflect the actual use of the piece; for example, a vase is used to house flowers so it was painted with dramatic and beautiful lifelike roses, or some other type of floral design. The design was then enhanced by adding luster, metallic, enamel, or pen work with ostentation and embellishment representative of the flamboyant lifestyles of the period, current movements, and fashion trends.

Some examples of this beautiful work include vases hand painted with pastel shades of blowsy rose blossoms so real looking you can see the dew on the petals; punch bowls and tankards with lush greenery and fruit so ripe you can smell the aroma; hand painted decorative plaques with men and women in romantic scenes that seduce and inspire our own private sweet dreams; elegant and erotic women, charming and beguiling children, naughty but endearing cherubs; beautiful and exotic birds with eye-catching feathers so detailed you can see the ripple of each quill; flamboyant fish, beloved and cherished pets, and wild and domesticated animals.

The American china painter had a passion for decorating pieces with roses—they were applied to vases, jardinières and punch bowls on separate bases, planters, and tea sets. Limoges pieces were painted with clusters of garden variety roses, cabbage roses, and giant velvety roses; some had abundant blossoms, some had petals loose and drenched in dew; some were enhanced with trailing vines of greenery like streamers. Other pieces were hand painted with rosebuds the color of pale peach and white blushed with pink, cream, lemon white, cotton candy pink, wine, and burgundy.

By the 1900s, there were over twenty-five thousand china painters in America and their artistic styles and abilities were as diverse as their numbers. When trying to identify a piece of Limoges decorated by an American china painter, keep in mind the styles, movements, and fashion trends of the period. Fruits or florals are the main subjects; the painting is naturalistic; a date or signature, if found, will be in script or block initials most likely on the bottom of the piece; and a factory mark backstamp will be present. For further insight by a china painter and author, *American Painted Porcelain* by Dorothy Kamm is very informative.

The Collector

Today, Limoges is still considered the Mecca for hard paste porcelain in France and there are approximately forty factories currently in production. Baccarat, Faberge, Hermes, Louis Vuitton, Daum, and Chanel are currently using the Limoges porcelain manufacturers. Table china, dinnerware sets, and Limoges boxes are just a few of the pieces still being produced for export to the United States at present. When in New York City, you can visit the Bernardaud Boutique on Park Avenue. New Limoges is sold in fine jewelry and gift stores, major department stores, catalogs, antique shops, and auction houses all over the world. Using the Internet, one can electronically order Limoges directly from France in a matter of seconds.

When Mary Frank Gaston's first edition of *The Collector's Encyclopedia of Limoges* was published in 1980, there were virtually no reproductions or fakes on the market. With her second book's release in 1996, she informed the collector of reproductions being imported to the United States from Taiwan. Since that time, collecting of Limoges porcelain has exploded in popularity. *Victoria Magazine* highlighted Limoges porcelain for their 4.1 million monthly readers in February 1997 and December 1999 in articles on Limoges Antiques Shop, Andover, Massachusetts. In 1999 an entire chapter was dedicated to "Collecting Limoges" in *The Business of Bliss, How to Profit From Doing What You Love*, published by the Hearst Publishing Company and featured on the Oprah Show.

This type of national exposure, along with web sites and Internet sales, has made Limoges sought after by new collectors and has also opened up opportunities for scam artists to sell inferior porcelain as Limoges. Unusual and desirable antique pieces have become a real scarcity for all levels of collectors and have allowed a window of opportunity for many reproductions with fake marks to be sold on the secondary market. It is a case of "buyer beware" and if you have a question about a mark that cannot be found, please contact a knowledgeable and reputable dealer. One of the most popular fake marks is the "ROC Limoges" mark selling on Internet auction sites. Any piece of porcelain with this mark is not fine hard paste porcelain from Limoges but rather a piece of inferior porcelain from the Republic of China. Faye Strumpf's book, *Limoges Boxes*, has an entire section dedicated to fake Limoges boxes and describes the fundamental differences between real and imitation markings.

An obsessed collector my entire life, I have spent most of my disposable income on antiques. As a disciplined collector, I educated myself reading books, visiting museums, and frequenting antique shops and shows in France, Europe, and the United States. As a passionate collector of Limoges, I purchased pieces that I loved and that were beautiful to me. I also wanted my Limoges art collection to be a form of investment. When purchasing a piece of Limoges, you should first and foremost love the piece. In addition, make sure the piece is in perfect condition with no chips, cracks, or repairs and that it is a marked piece of Limoges. If the piece was hand painted in the factory, a French artist signature and an overglaze decorating mark are desirable.

The most desired Limoges pieces are the large and unusual blanks, sets, scarce or unusual pieces, pieces well painted in detail, signed by the artist, with older and rare marks, and in pristine condition. Limoges pieces hand painted in the French and American decorating factories and artist signed are by far the best investment pieces. Decorative pieces hand painted by amateur American artists are the most appealing to a majority of collectors and this has been reflected in their prices and accounts for their drastic increase in value over the past ten years. An amateur American artist signature should not affect the price or desirability of a piece, as most of these artists are not recognized and are untraceable. The largest price differential is between a piece of porcelain decorated in the transfer ware technique versus that of a hand painted piece. Unless the art on the hand painted piece is so unaesthetic that it makes the piece undesirable, most hand painted pieces sell at higher prices. But, even the most undesirable piece of Limoges will sell at auction or on an Internet auction site.

Purchasing a unique piece of Limoges is as individual as each of us. Keep in mind the characteristics noted above that affect the value of a piece (size, unusual blank, well painted with a factory artist signature, factory mark, and condition) and then purchase what you love. Plenty of Limoges is available in every variety, from many factories, decorated with diversity, and in price ranges for all levels of collectors and investors. In addition, there are many reasons to purchase a piece of Limoges—from inspiration to investment, diversion to decoration. Whatever the reason, living with your Limoges collection—whether in a dorm in Korea or a Victorian home in New England—provides a perfect complement for any home and will enhance your life and inspire your imagination.

Part II

Living with Your Limoges

The Front Hall, Entrance, Parlor, or Foyer

A formal entryway, parlor, foyer or vestibule sets the tone for a collector's emphasis. Entrances are as unique as the individual and are a great place to focus on pieces that are particularly special to that collector. Entrances can evoke a mood and call attention to that special piece of fine Limoges art.

Antiques, accessories, art, and Limoges placed together provide the appeal of informal balance that many of us hire a decorator to achieve. Several pieces of Limoges displayed as a group call attention to a favorite piece but serve as a single composition. Limoges vases organized by symmetrical arrangement or placed according to color make dramatic statements.

A fireplace with an overmantel, a second mantel shelf, is suitable for the exhibition of carefully chosen Limoges pieces. A pair of Limoges urns or matching vases can promote feelings of stateliness and balance suited for a more formal entrance. Paintings on Limoges porcelain, chargers, and plaques hung on entry walls or staircase walls create grand and formal entrances evoking the atmosphere of a museum. Relying on a few helpful principles—such as using odd numbers and varying heights and shapes—will help you compose vignettes of Limoges that are both pleasing and personal in an entrance.

Unique vase, 14" tall with wonderful gold gilt elephant handles. Hand painted with roses, artist signed "Mrs CW Lamson, Erie, PA" and dated March 16, 1905. Underglaze factory mark in green, D & Co., France, Délinières & Co., Mark 3, ca. 1894-1900. $1,200-$1,600.

Reverse side of vase.

Opposite page: A formal Victorian entryway leads into a parlor that showcases massive pieces of Limoges.

Vase, 14" x 10" at the base. Underglaze factory mark in green, "PM DE M" monogrammed with "Limoges, France," Mavaleix factory mark, ca. 1908-1914. Overglaze decorating mark in green, crown with "Coronet," Borgfeldt Mark 1, ca. 1906-1920, factory artist "Rouncon." Import paper mark "Owen Moore and Co., Portland, Maine." $1,800-$2,500.

This Victorian fireplace, in working condition with original cherry mantel and mirror, is perfect for showcasing a diversity of Limoges art: vases, jardinières, plaques, chargers, platters, and trays.

Top center: The overmantel serves as the perfect shelf for a pair of stately Limoges urns. The pair act as matching bookends to this wonderful oil on canvas, artist signed and dated 1903.

Limoges vases organized by symmetrical arrangement and placed according to color make a dramatic statement in this entryway.

Jardinière, 12" x 14" gold gilt lion head handles, base with four feet hand painted with roses. Underglaze factory mark in green, D&Co., Délinières & Co., Mark 3, ca. 1894-1900. $3,500-$4,500.

A Victorian silk shawl is the perfect canvas for this magnificent Limoges jardinière.

Pair of vases, 22" tall bolted to base. Hand painted roses, neck and base enameled with raised gold gilt. Underglaze factory mark in green, W.G.&Co., France, Guérin Mark 2, ca. 1891-1900. $2,800-$3,000 each.

Charger, 18" diameter in original frame. Underglaze factory mark in green, T&V Limoges France, Tressemann & Vogt Mark 7, ca. 1892-1907. $700-$900.

Tray with handles, 14" diameter. Underglaze factory mark in green, T&V France, Tressemann & Vogt Mark 5a, ca. 1892-1907. $300-$400.

Large platter, 20" long x 14" wide. Underglaze factory mark in green, H&Co. with initial "L" and France, Haviland & Co Mark H, ca. 1888-1896. $2,000-$2,500.

Painting on porcelain, 15" diameter in original frame. Underglaze factory mark in green, Déposé Touraine, T&V France, Tressemann & Vogt Mark 5a, ca. 1892-1907. $800-$1,000.

Painting on porcelain, 9" diameter in original frame. Underglaze factory mark in green, J.P.L., Jean Pouyat Mark 1, ca. 1851-1875. $1,200-$1,600.

Plaque, 14" diameter, pierced holes in back of blank. Underglaze factory mark in green, Limoges France in flag with bird, Charles Martin & Duche Mark 1, ca. after 1891. $800-$900.

Large, 18" tall Limoges vase with ornate gold handles. Unmarked, artist's initials "LHT" and dated 1904. $1,200-$1,700.

Urn, 14" tall with gold branch style handles that split, unique stopper painted gold. Underglaze factory mark in green, W.G.& Co. Limoges France, William Guérin Mark 2, ca. 1900-1932. $1,000-$1,200.

Vase, 9" tall with gold handles that split into three sections., hand painted and enameled designs, artist dated 1890. Underglaze factory mark in green, J.P.L. France, Jean Pouyat Mark 5, ca. 1890-1932. $500-$700.

Vase, 16" tall with handles, unmarked blank attributed to Limoges. $1,300-$1,600.

Vase, 16" tall with hand painted cascading roses and gold rim, artist signed "L. Haste." Underglaze factory mark in green, T&V Limoges France, Tressemann & Vogt Mark 7, ca. 1892-1907. $2,200-$2,500.

Vase, rose bowl, 7.5" tall, artist's initials "M.W." on bottom. Underglaze factory mark in green, J.P.L. France, Jean Pouyat Mark 5, ca. 1890-1932. Import mark, under the glaze in green L.Cooley with a line followed by Boston (U.S.A.). $200-$400.

Vase, 15.5" tall, five panels with hand painted roses on outside and interior of rim, artist signed "Hicks K." Underglaze factory mark in green, B&Co., France, Bernardaud & Co. Mark 1, ca. 1900-1914. $2,000-$2,5000.

Vase, 9.5" tall, serpent shaped handles with roses. Underglaze factory mark in green, J.P.L. France, Jean Pouyat Mark 5, ca. 1890-1932. $550-$750.

Limoges lamp, 16" tall. Underglaze factory mark in green, J.P.L. France, Jean Pouyat Mark 5, ca. 1890-1932. $475-$700.

Reverse of vase.

Tiny vestibule adjoining a lovely staircase. A gold gilt, marble top statue is the perfect perch for a Limoges punch bowl with cherubs hand painted inside the bowl.

Dark Victorian wallpaper wraps its arms around you and is the perfect canvas for pieces of hand painted art on Limoges porcelain that complement the large Limoges punch bowl.

Mammoth Limoges punch bowl, 13" x 26" diameter, underglaze factory mark in green, J.P.L. France, Jean Pouyat Mark 5, ca. 1890-1932. $1,500-$2,500.

Limoges punch bowl on base, 13.75" diameter with separate base. Hand painted with grapes and cherubs. Underglaze factory mark in green, T&V Limoges France, Tressemann & Vogt, Mark 7, ca. 1892-1907. $2,000-$3,000.

Limoges painting on porcelain, 9" x 12" with hand painted roses. Underglaze factory mark in green, T&V Limoges France, Tressemann & Vogt Mark 7, ca. 1892-1907. $1,200-$1,500.

A grand staircase calls for massed pieces of Limoges art in ornate gilt frames. A pair of nineteenth century French needlepoint chairs make the perfect bookends for this nineteenth century French ladies writing desk.

A different view of the staircase.

Staircase with massed collection of hand painted Limoges on porcelain in original frames.

Large painting on porcelain, 21" x 24" in original frame, artist signed "G. Asselineau." Underglaze factory mark in green, W.G&Co., France, William Guérin Mark 2, ca. 1891-1900. $2,500-$3,500.

Painting on porcelain, 12.5" x 17" in original frame, illegible artist's signature and dated 1889. Underglaze factory mark in green, T&V Limoges, Tressemann & Vogt Mark 4b, ca. 1892-1907. $2,000-$2,500.

Painting on porcelain, 17" x 18" in original frame, signed "a' Paroy." Underglaze factory mark in green, T&V Limoges, Tressemann & Vogt Mark 4b, ca. 1892-1907. $2,000-$2,500.

Painting on porcelain, 17" x 19" in original frame, artist's initials "J.B." Unusual hand painted Egyptian scene of three women at market. Underglaze factory mark in green, D.&Co. France, Délinières & Co. Mark 3, ca. 1894-1900. $1,200-$1,500.

Pair of paintings on porcelain, 12" x 12" hand painted desert scenes. Underglaze factory mark in green, T&V Limoges, Tressemann & Vogt Mark 4b, ca. 1892-1907. Pair $1,000-$2,200.

Large painting on porcelain, 14" x 17" of a woman with musical instruments, artist signed "Ann" and dated 1898. Underglaze factory mark in green, T&V Limoges France, T&V Tressemann & Vogt Mark 7, ca. 1892-1907. $1,200-$1,400.

Large oval painting on porcelain, 24" diameter in original frame. Underglaze factory mark in green, W.G.&Co. France, William Guérin Mark 2, ca. 1891-1900. $3,500-$5,500.

Painting on porcelain, 12" x 17" in original frame, Parisian scene. Underglaze factory mark in green, J.P.L. France, Jean Pouyat Mark 5, ca. 1890-1932. $2,000-$2,200.

Enter this formal entryway through leaded glass doors and be greeted by an unusual Limoges vase sitting next to a fabulous bronze sculpture.

Painting on porcelain, 11" x 14" with figural scene of woman and cherub. Underglaze factory mark in green, T&V France, Tressemann & Vogt Mark 5a, ca. 1892-1907. $500-$1,000.

Center vase, 11" tall with ornate gold gilt handles. Underglaze factory mark in green, W.G. & Co., France, William Guérin Mark 2, ca. 1891-1900. $900-$1,500.

Huge double doors lead into this luscious entryway and staircase leading to the living areas. A beautiful dated and artist signed piece of hand painted art on Limoges porcelain with original frame is amongst the greenery.

In this entryway stands a nineteenth century vitrine holding a collection of Limoges with unique pieces painted colors that complement the warm dark cranberry wallpaper.

Hand painted Limoges porcelain in original frame, 26" x 24" with artist's initial "LLK" and dated 1901. Underglaze factory mark in green, T & V Limoges France, Tressemann & Vogt Mark 7, ca. 1892-1907. $1,500-$2,000.A

Vase, 13" tall with pink and red roses. Underglaze factory mark in green, PP, LA SEYNIE, Paroutaud Freres, Mark 1, ca. 1903-1917. $700-$900.

Vase, 12" tall unusual blank. Underglaze factory mark in green, PL Limoges France, La Porcelaine Limousine Mark 1, ca. 1905-late 1930s. $800-$900.

Tray, 12" diameter with heavy gold gilt rim with hand painted roses. Underglaze factory mark in green, Haviland France, Mark I, ca. 1894-1931. $275-$475.

Small pitcher or creamer, 5" from spout to handle. Underglaze factory mark in green, Limoges France, Mark 2, after 1891. $75-$125.

Basket, 8" with handle and multi colored roses. Underglaze factory mark in green, Limoges in a star with Limoges, France, Coiffe Mark 3, ca. 1891-1914. Overglaze exporting mark in red, LS & S Limoges France, Lewis Straus & Sons Mark, ca. 1890s-1920s. $175-$275.

Bowl with under plate for mayo, "E. Miler" signature. Underglaze factory mark in green, T&V France, Tressemann & Vogt, Mark 5a., ca. 1892-1907. $375-$475.

Pitcher, 7" with "E. Miler" signature. Underglaze factory mark in green, J.P.L. France, Jean Pouyat Mark 5, ca. 1891-1932. $475-$625.

Luncheon set, 8.5" plate, cup and saucer, "E. Miler" signature. Underglaze factory mark in green, T&V France, Century Patent Feb 1904, Tressemann & Vogt Mark 5a, ca. 1892-1907. $225-$275 each place setting.

Pitcher, 7" with hand painted blackberries. Underglaze factory mark in green, J.P.L. France, Jean Pouyat Mark 5, ca. 1891-1932. $475-$625.

Chocolate pot with violets, 10" tall. Underglaze factory mark in green, J.P.L. France, Jean Pouyat Mark 5, ca. 1891-1932. $350-$450.

Chocolate pot, 7.5" tall with hand painted pansies. Underglaze factory mark in green, W.G.&Co., Limoges France, William Guérin Mark 3, ca. 1900-1932. $250-$275.

Chocolate pot, 12" tall with hand painted irises. Underglaze factory mark in green, with a star and Limoges France, Coiffe Mark 3, ca. 1891-1914. $595-$695.

Bowl, 12" diameter with hand painted violets, heavy gilt. Underglaze factory mark in green, T&V Limoges France, Tressemann & Vogt, Mark 7, ca. 1892-1907. $595-$795.

Relish dish, 16" across. Underglaze factory mark in green, T&V Limoges France, Tressemann & Vogt, Mark 7, ca. 1892-1907. $225-$275.

Bowl, 4" with hand painted pansies. Underglaze factory mark in green, T&V France, Tressemann & Vogt, Mark 5a, ca. 1892-1907. $75-$95.

This formal entry looks like a wall in a local museum of fine art. Original paintings on Limoges porcelain are nestled amongst original pieces of art and a French nineteenth century framed needlepoint.

Painting on porcelain, 16" tall x 12.5" wide. Made up of four individual enhanced transfer pieces on porcelain 6" x 5" each, artist's initials "HFM" bottom left corner. This is the famous Four Seasons "Winter, Spring, Summer, Fall" decoration of Victorian women seen on many other pieces of porcelain decorated in Europe. Underglaze factory mark in green, W.G.&Co., Limoges France, William Guérin Mark 3, ca. 1900-1932. $2,500-$4,000.

"Winter" painting on porcelain.

"Spring" painting on porcelain

"Summer" painting on porcelain.

Top center: Painting on porcelain, 8" oval. Underglaze factory mark in green, W.G.&Co., Limoges France, William Guérin Mark 3, ca. 1900-1932. $600-$800.

Top right: Painting on porcelain, 7" x 5", woman sitting on moon with owl in original ornate frame. Underglaze factory mark in green, W.G.&Co., Limoges France, William Guérin Mark 3, ca. 1900-1932. $600-$800.

"Fall" painting on porcelain.

Painting on porcelain, 10" x 18", Victorian children playing, artist signed "Dubois." Underglaze factory mark in green, W.G.&Co., Limoges France, William Guérin Mark 3, ca. 1900-1932. $3,500-$4,500.

Painting on porcelain, 17" x 15". Underglaze factory mark in green, T&V France, Mark 5a, ca. 1892-1907. $2,200-$2,500.

Top left: Painting on porcelain, 11" x 8.5". Underglaze factory mark in green, T&V Limoges France, Tressemann & Vogt Mark 7, ca. 1892-1907. $1,000-$1,200.

Top center: Painting on porcelain, 16" x 12". Underglaze factory mark in green, T&V France, Tressemann & Vogt Mark 5a, ca. 1892-1907. $2,200-$2,500.

Painting on porcelain, 10" x 12". Underglaze factory mark in green, T&V France, Tressemann & Vogt Mark 5a, ca. 1892-1907. Artist signed, front bottom right corner, "F.L. Smith." $2,000-$2,400.

Top left: Painting on porcelain, 7.5" x 5.5". Underglaze factory mark in green, T&V Limoges France, Tressemann & Vogt Mark 7, ca. 1892-1907. $600-$800.

Top center: Painting on porcelain, 4" x 5.5". Underglaze factory mark in green, T&V Limoges France, Tressemann & Vogt Mark 7, ca. 1892-1907. $450-$600.

Bottom left: Painting on porcelain, 7.5" x 5.5". Underglaze factory mark in green, T&V Limoges France, Tressemann & Vogt Mark 7, ca. 1892-1907. $600-$800.

Bottom right: Painting on porcelain, 13" x 15.5", hand painted tropical orchids attributed to American artist Martin Johnson Heade. Underglaze factory mark in green, T&V Limoges France, Tressemann & Vogt Mark 7, ca. 1892-1907. $1,500-$2,500.

Tea Time

"The tea ritual feels safe, comforting, and inviting. Quietly and without threat, it calls us out of ourselves and into relationships. Even the tea itself—warm and sweet and comforting—inspires a feeling of relaxation and trust that fosters shared confidences."
—Emilie Barnes

For at least two centuries, the Emilie Barnes saying "Come for Tea" has been just another way of saying "Come, let's share a little bit of our lives together."

The art of taking afternoon tea is especially delightful when the cup of tea shared together is served out of an elegant Limoges teapot and poured into a dainty hand painted Limoges teacup. In recent years Americans have adopted this gracious custom, but tea was, in fact, introduced to Europe in the sixteenth century. France and Germany had brief flings with tea drinking, while England, Russia, and Holland really took to the custom. In the mid 1700s, the tea craze in England gave rise to magnificent landscaped tea gardens, where the fashionable would gather to take tea, share gossip, see, and be seen. By the end of the 1700s, tea gardens lost most of their popularity and tea drinking became more of an at home event. Anna, Duchess of Bedford, is credited with the custom of afternoon tea as it is known today, but it was Queen Victoria who set the standard of elegance and ostentation for the art of afternoon tea.

During her reign, Queen Victoria visited France frequently, and it was during these visits that she was greeted with gifts of Sevres and Limoges porcelain from the King of France. Overwhelmed with sentiment, emotional attachment, and the fact that each gift was a beautiful piece of art on porcelain, she acquired a large array of Limoges. Queen Victoria loved ostentatious vases suited for a castle, detailed Limoges boxes that held her children's baby teeth, and tea time accouterments, making all of these pieces very popular during the Victorian era.

Afternoon tea was seen as an art. There were elaborate table settings with lovely linens and sterling silver teaspoons. Tea was served in elegant porcelain teapots, with matching cups and saucers displayed on hand painted gold gilded trays. Matching dessert and cake plates were commonplace. Large ostentatious sugar bowls (due to the high cost of sugar, a large bowl was proof of one's wealth), biscuit jars with elaborate handles, and lovely hand painted tea strainers with under liners were proudly on display during an afternoon tea.

Should you visit New England, a visit to the Wenham Tea House in Wenham, Massachusetts, will be a treat. This charming institution is the oldest known tea house in the United States today. An intimate afternoon tea consists of the traditional cup of hot tea with milk and a clove studded lemon wedge, followed by fancy tea sandwiches, delicious homemade scones, and desserts. To quote Sydney Smith: "What would the world do without Tea? How did it exist? I am glad I was not born before tea."

Tea set: teapot, 7" tall with matching sugar and creamer, hand painted an unusual green with raised gold paste decoration, artist's initials "E.N.B." Underglaze factory mark in green, J.P.L. France, Jean Pouyat, Mark 7, ca. 1891-1932; tray, 12" diameter. Underglaze white ware mark in green, T&V Limoges, Tressemann & Vogt, Mark 4, ca. 1892-1907. Set $1,200-1,500.

Tea set: teapot, 5.25" tall; creamer, 4" tall; sugar, 4.75" tall; tray, 12" diameter. Underglaze factory mark in green, J.P.L., Jean Pouyat Mark 3, ca. 1876-1890. Set $800-$1,000.

Teapot, 4.75" tall. Underglaze factory mark in green, Haviland & Co., Mark I, ca. 1894-1931. $350-$450.

Tea set: teapot, sugar, creamer, with matching cups and saucers. Set marked in green, W.G.&Co., William Guérin Mark 2, ca. 1891-1900. $450-$640.

Tea set: teapot, 4.5" tall; sugar, 3.75" tall; creamer, 2.5" tall. Hand painted heavy gold with insets of a floral design. Set $395-$495.

Top left: Teapot, 4.5" tall. Underglaze factory mark in green, Haviland & Co., Mark I, ca. 1894-1931. $225-$300.

Top right: Coffee pot, 8" tall. This pot is the subject in an original artwork by John Lundquist named "Limoges." Underglaze factory mark in green, Limoges France Mark 6, ca. after 1891. $350-$450.

Bottom left: Coffee pot, 8.5" tall. Underglaze factory mark in green, W.G.&Co., Limoges France, William Guérin Mark 3, ca. after 1900-1932. $350-$450.

Bottom right: Tea set: pot, sugar, creamer, with matching tray. All marked in green: J.P.L. France, Jean Pouyat Mark 5, ca. 1891-1932. Set $800-$1,000.

Tea set: pot, sugar, creamer, with matching tray. All marked in green: D&C France, Délinières Company, Mark 3, ca. 1894-1900. Set $800-$1,200.

Tea set: pot, sugar, creamer, cups and saucers. All marked in green: T&V France, Tressemann & Vogt Mark 5a, ca. 1892-1907. Set $800-$1,000.

Tea set: pot, sugar, creamer, with matching tray. All marked in green: Venice T&V France, Tressemann & Vogt Mark 5c, ca. 1892-1907. Set $900-$1,400.

Tea set: pot, 6" tall, with sugar, creamer, and matching tray. All marked in green: AK France, Klingenberg Mark 7, ca. 1890s-1910. Set $500-$800.

Top left: Tea set: pot, sugar, creamer, with matching tray. All marked in green: J.P.L. France, Jean Pouyat Mark 5, 1891-1932. Set $500-$800.

Bottom left: Tea set: pot, 7.5" tall, with matching sugar, creamer, and four matching cups and saucers, artist signed "C.Wynn" and dated 1901. Set marked in green: T&V France Déposé, Tressemann & Vogt, Mark 6, ca. 1892-1907. Set 800-$1,000.

Top right: Teapot, 3.5" tall. Underglaze factory mark in green, J.P.L. France, Jean Pouyat Mark 5, ca. 1891-1932. $275-$375.

Center right: Teapot, 4" tall. Underglaze factory mark in green, W.G.&Co., Limoges France, William Guérin Mark 3, ca. after 1900-1932. $275-$375.

Teapot, 4" tall. Underglaze factory mark in green, Mavaleix , P.M. ca. 1908-1914. Overglaze decorating mark, Coronet, George Borgfeldt Mark 1, ca. 1906-1920. $275-$375.

Teapot, 6" tall. Unique hand painted pot with gold and roses all around and inside the pot. Impressed white ware mark, AK, Klingenberg Mark 3, ca. 1880s-1890. Artist's initials "KLR" and dated 1890. $600-$700.

Covered jar, 7.5" tall. Underglaze factory mark in green, H&Co., Mark E, ca. 1877. $195-$295.

Inside of teapot.

This romantic table set for tea includes various tea time accoutrements of Limoges porcelain on a beautiful handmade needlepoint rug used as a table covering.

Teapot, 3.5" x 4.5", artist's initials "J.M.B." Underglaze factory mark in green, B&C Limoges France, Bernardaud & Company Mark 3, ca. 1914-1930s and after. $125-$225.

Biscuit or cracker jar, 7.5" tall. Underglaze factory mark in green, T&V Limoges France, Tressemann & Vogt, Mark 10, ca. 1892-1907. $250-$350.

Vase, 12" tall. Underglaze factory mark in green, J.P.L. France, Pouyat Mark 7, ca. 1890-1932. $1,200-$1,500.

Tea tray with handles, 16" diameter, artist's initial "B." Underglaze factory mark in green, T&V Limoges France, Tressemann & Vogt, Mark 10, ca. 1892-1907. $550-$750.

Hand painted dessert set for twelve: plates, 8.5" and 7.5" diameter. Underglaze factory mark in green, Haviland France, Mark I, ca. 1894-1931: cup and saucer, underglaze factory mark in green, GDA, Gérard, Dufraisseix, and Abbot, Mark 1, ca. 1900-1941. Set $1,800-2,300.

Tea strainer with underliner or drip bowl. Underglaze factory mark in green, T&V Limoges France, Tressemann & Vogt Mark 7, ca. 1892-1907. Set $295-$395.

Letter holder, 6.5" tall x 8" wide, artist signed "C.L. Howard." Underglaze factory mark in green, Limoges France, Mark 1, ca. 1891 and after. $275-$375.

Tea tray, 12" x 11". Underglaze factory mark in green, AK, Klingenberg, Mark 1, ca. 1880s-1890. $250-$350.

Dessert plate, 7.5" diameter with matching cup and saucer. Underglaze factory mark in green, J.P.L. France, Jean Pouyat, Mark 7, ca. 1891-1932. Set of six, $395-495.

Tea and toast, dessert, or sandwich tray set. One of a set of six, this one has hand painted poppy cookies courtesy of Yummy Mummy Cookie Factory, Andover, Massachusetts. Underglaze factory mark in green, W.G.&Co., Limoges France, William Guérin Mark 3, ca. after 1900-1932. $175-$275 each.

Wonderful tea and toast or sandwich tray with matching cup. Underglaze factory mark in green, W.G.&Co., William Guérin Mark 3, ca. after 1900-1932. $100-$125.

Tea and toast, dessert, or sandwich tray with footed cup. Underglaze factory mark in green, T&V France Depose, Tressemann & Vogt Mark 6, ca. 1892-1907, probably about 1900. $100-$125.

Tea and toast, dessert, or sandwich tray. One of set of six, each hand painted with a different floral pattern. Underglaze factory mark in green, D&C France, Délinières and Company Mark 3, ca. 1894-1900. $100-$125 each.

Unique tea and toast or dessert set, plate 9" diameter. Underglaze factory mark in green, T&V Limoges, Tressemann & Vogt, Mark 4b, ca. 1892-1907, but probably before Mark 5a. $200-$225.

Tea set on a tea cart is ready for service. Set is partially marked with underglaze factory mark in green, T&V Limoges, Tressemann & Vogt Mark 4, ca. 1892-1907. Set $350-$400.

Cake plate, 11.5", and matching dessert plates make a beautiful statement on a white wall. Underglaze factory mark in green, T&V Limoges, Tressemann & Vogt Mark 4, ca. 1892-1907. Set $275-$375.

Cake plate, 11.5" diameter. Underglaze factory mark in green, T&V Limoges France Déposé, Tressemann & Vogt Mark 8, ca. 1907-1919. $225-$275.

Center: Cake plate, 11" diameter. Underglaze factory mark in green, W.G.&Co., Limoges France, William Guérin Mark 3, ca. after 1900-1932. $225-$275.

Right: Cake plate, 11" diameter. Underglaze factory mark in green, T&V Limoges, Tressemann & Vogt Mark 4b, ca. 1892-1907, probably prior to Mark 5a. $225-$275.

Left: Cake plate, 11.5" diameter. Underglaze factory mark in green, Haviland France, Mark I, ca. 1894-1931. $295-$395.

Right: Cake plate, 11.5" diameter, artist's initials "A.A.E." and dated 1909. Underglaze factory mark, Haviland France, Mark I, ca. 1894-1931. $295-$395.

Left: Cake plate, 11.5" diameter. Underglaze factory mark in green, B&C France, Bernardaud & Co., Mark 1, ca. 1900-1914. Picard decorating mark in gold emblem. $550-$650.

Right: Dessert plate, 11" diameter, artist signed "McMillan." Underglaze factory mark in green, T&V Limoges, Tressemann & Vogt Mark 4, ca. 1892-1907. $225-$300.

Large cake plate or serving piece, 16" circumference, artist signed on front "March." Underglaze factory mark in green, Déposé Touraine T&V France, Tressemann & Vogt Mark 8.1, ca. 1892-1907. $750-$950.

Dessert or truffle plate, 11" square, artist's initials "M.E.H." and dated 1898. Underglaze and impressed white ware mark in green, Limoges AL with anchor and France, Lanternier Mark 4, ca. 1891-1914. $375-$475.

Cake plate, 12" diameter. Underglaze factory mark in green, three stars Limoges France, Plainemaison Mark, ca. 1890s-1910. Overglaze decorating mark, Coronet, Borgfeldt Mark 1, ca. 1906-1920. $175-$200.

Cake plate on pedestal, 4" x 12" diameter. Underglaze factory mark in green, T&V Limoges France Depose, Tressemann & Vogt, Mark 8, ca. 1907-1919. $295-$395.

Dessert set for twelve includes cake plate, 11.5" diameter; ice cream serving platter, 13" x 8"; dessert plate or ice cream dish, 6.5" with matching cup and saucer. Each piece is artist signed "J.J. Driscoll" and dated 1910. Underglaze factory mark in green, T&V Limoges France Depose, Tressemann & Vogt, Mark 8, ca. 1907-1919. Set $1,800-$2,300.

Top right: Lovely Pairpoint teacup sits amongst a collection of sterling tussie mussies, also known as posey holders or nosegays. Typically made of gold, silver, silverplate, cut steel, horn, ivory, enamel on tin, silver gilt, brass, shell, glass, mother-of-pearl, and hand painted porcelain.

Bottom right: A Limoges tussie mussie sits on this tea table waiting for its mistress to pick it up before she leaves. Meanwhile, it is a lovely addition to the tea table.

Right: Rare porcelain tussie mussie marked AK France, Klingenberg Mark 7, ca. 1890s-1910. $395-$495.

The Living Room

Contemporary all white living room is made dramatic with splashes of cranberry accessories.

The living room is a great place to highlight your Limoges art. A fireplace, if one is present, is almost always the focal point of this room. Think of accessorizing the mantel and the wall space around and above the fireplace with pieces of Limoges. Porcelain makes impressive groupings when colors harmonize, sizes are varied, and pieces are integrated with other types of art. A painting overhanging the mantle that echoes the theme of the Limoges gives the power of subtle repetition and has a powerful visual impact. Reoccurring shapes such as a round mirror or a bulbous Limoges vase or jardinière are successful elements of great style and will make your fireplace a unique focal point in your living room.

Large living spaces with high ceilings call for large scale Limoges art work. A large collection is most effective when massed. Diverse art collections become unified when displayed on a dark wall covering and create an individual approach to displaying Limoges. A few special pieces or a single large piece of Limoges will make a bigger impression if you isolate them for impact.

Using upholstered furniture pieces and porcelain pieces in the same colors, even in small doses, is a great unifier, pulling together disparate elements and making a room feel complete. Neutral fabrics provide tranquility and will enhance dark, dramatic Limoges pieces. Combining fabrics softens the formality of a room and provides a wide range of possibilities for Limoges accessories in many colors. Color helps generate and create visual interest—and Limoges porcelain comes in all colors on the spectrum.

The cozy effects of beamed ceilings and smaller living areas create more intimate settings. Serious Limoges collectors should think carefully about how to display their collections for maximum use of space and visual impact. A rosy alcove can be created by using a vase hand painted with roses to complement the fabric in the room. A Limoges bowl with striking interior painting works well on a low surface such as a coffee table. Placing a special

The contemporary fireplace mantel is a perfect perch for a collection of Limoges vases and the coffee table makes an elegant setting for a cup of tea.

Limoges piece on a stand elicits interest and conversation. Collections displayed in French vitrines and hung in groupings on walls and over door moldings make use of limited space while showcasing each piece of Limoges and illuminating a distinct decorating style.

A pair of 9" tall, double handled Limoges vases stand like bookends on both sides of an American Belleek vase. The vases have the underglazed Jean Pouyat Mark 5, ca. 1891-1932. $450-$650 each.

A beautiful hand painted vitrine houses a lovely collection of porcelain.

A Limoges bon-bon covered bowl sits on top of a lovely cherry candlestick stand.

A lovely Limoges pitcher, bowl, and cider pitcher, artist signed on the front by listed French artists, sit on the top shelf. All three pieces have both the factory underglaze mark and the decorating overglaze mark on the back. On the second shelf are complementary Limoges pieces hand painted by amateur American artists. Pitcher $595-$795; bowl $495-$695; cider pitcher $595-$695; other pieces $500-$900 each.

A nineteenth century French vitrine provides the perfect display cabinet for a beloved collection that complements this lovely Limoges tea set.

Three piece tea set with matching tray. Artist signed "F. Magy" and all pieces have the underglaze factory mark in green, W.G.&Co., France, William Guérin Mark 2, ca. 1891-1900. Set $900-$1500.

Top left: A large modern living room is accessorized with Limoges lamps, trays, vases, planters, and a tea set.

Top right: In the corner, on top of a nineteenth century inlaid chest, is a magnificent Limoges vase. It has ornate handles with heavy gold gilt and a reserve with a hand painted scene of a man courting a woman. Underglaze factory mark in green, W.G.&Co., Limoges France, William Guérin Mark 3, ca. 1900-1932. $2,000-$3,000.

Bottom left: On the hearth of this fireplace is a most unusual Limoges jardinière. Underglaze factory mark in green, W.G.&Co., France, William Guérin Mark 2, ca. 1891-1900. $2,000-$3,000.

Bottom right: This lovely Limoges tea set and matching tray are marked W.G.&Co., William Guérin Mark 2, ca. 1891-1900. Set $900-$1,500.

Rare ewer, 11" tall, reserves are hand painted with figural scenes. One of the reserves has a signature and date, "A. Nice 1893," in brown. Underglaze factory mark H. & Co., Haviland Mark 11, ca. 1888-1896 and "H.&Co." written in gold script. $2,000-$2,200.

Close-up of hand painted reserves on the ewer.

H. & Co. underglaze mark on the ewer, with "H. & Co." also written in gold script.

Rare tea caddy, 9" tall, with hand painted Victorian woman in a raised gold gilt reserve. Back has a hand painted scene with lovers in a canoe. Bottom states: "November 16th 1898, M.R.W. to H.B.G." Underglaze factory mark in green, CA France Déposé, Charles J. Ahrenfeldt Mark 6, ca. 1894-1930s. $400-$900.

Vase, 6.5" x 9.5" rare blank. Underglaze factory mark in green, T&V Limoges France, Tressemann & Vogt Mark 7, ca. 1892-1907. $700-$800.

Top left: This lovely fireplace is in the E. Sibbill Banks House, built in Waltham, Massachusetts in 1892. On the National Register of Historic Places, this home is an excellent example of the vernacular Queen Anne. The fireplace surround is of American Majolica tile, most likely from Chelsea, Massachusetts (J. & J.G. Low Art Tile). These tiles are done in high relief and in the middle top of this surround is a beautiful cameo profile of a lovely lady done in a soft apricot bisque glaze.

Bottom left: The mantel houses favorite pieces of Limoges that provide balance to the portrait overhanging the mantel and the nineteenth century French bisque bust.

A modern living room with a brick fireplace creates the perfect backdrop for large pieces of Limoges that are used to house various tropical plants.

Punch bowl with base, 13" x 8.5", houses a seasonal house plant. Underglaze factory mark in green, T&V Limoges France, Tressemann & Vogt Mark 7, ca. 1892-1907. $2,000-$3,000.

Left: Jardinière with base, 9.5" x 13", heavily gilded with handles shaped in the form of lions' heads. Underglaze factory mark in green, D&Co., Délinières Mark 3, ca. 1894-1900. $3,000-$3,500.

Right: Punch bowl, 13" x 6", with mixtion decoration. Underglaze factory mark in green, T&V Limoges France, Tressemann and Vogt Mark 7, ca. 1892-1907. Overglaze decorating mark in purple, Tressemann & Vogt Mark 9, ca. 1892-1907. $800-$1,000.

This Victorian couch wraps around you and is the perfect complement for the Limoges paintings on porcelain on the wall and the collection of vases in the room.

Nice collection of various Limoges paintings on porcelain, signed by the artists. All have the underglaze mark in green T&V Limoges France, Tressemann & Vogt Mark 9, ca. 1892-1907. Prices range from $700-$2,500.

Vase, 12" tall, with artist's initials in script and dated 1907. Underglaze factory mark in green, W.G.&Co., Limoges France, William Guérin Mark 3, ca. 1900-1932. $800-$1,200.

Vase, 12.5" tall, signed "Aunt Mary, April 3, 1909." Underglaze factory mark in green, D&C France, Délinières & Co. Mark 3, ca. 1894-1900. $500-$600.

Vase, 8" tall, artist signed "I.H. Jewett" and dated 1907. Underglaze factory mark in green, D&C France, Délinières & Co. Mark 3, ca. 1894-1900. This vase is an example of the blank being decorated several years after production. $400-$495.

Unusual vase with separate base, 12.5" tall. Underglaze factory mark in green, J.P.L., Jean Pouyat Mark 3, ca. 1862-1900. $2,000-$2,200.

Vase, 9.5" tall, with gold handles. Underglaze factory mark in green, J.P.L. France, Jean Pouyat Mark 5, ca. 1891-1932. $800-$900.

A comfortable living room with needlepoint screen, rug, and coffee table harmonize with unique Limoges accessories that have complementary colors.

Large punch bowl, 9" x 17", with underglaze factory mark in green, J.P.L., Jean Pouyat Mark 3, ca. 1862-1900. With poppies painted inside, this piece makes a dramatic statement when positioned on a coffee table. $3,000-$3,500.

Unusual painting of turkeys on porcelain, artist's initials and dated 1907. Underglaze factory mark in green, T&V Limoges France, Tressemann & Vogt Mark 7, ca. 1892-1907. $1,200-$1,500.

Outside of the same punch bowl on a matching tray.

Formal Victorian living room with high ceilings is accessorized with large pieces of Limoges. Jardinières, lamps, and vases sit on French side tables. A rare 1920s coffee table with original gray marble and Limoges hand painted floral inserts is the focal point.

A large Victorian milk glass topped table in the corner is perfect for this wonderful jardinière. Beautiful chargers are hung around the nineteenth century Venetian glass mirror.

Close-up of two of the twenty original floral inserts surrounded by ormolu that trim the 1920s coffee table. Each is hand painted with a unique floral scene.

Large, 28" tall lamp has raised gold and a unique Oriental motif of an enameled dragon. Underglaze factory mark in green, W.G.&Co., France, William Guérin Mark 2, ca. 1891-1900. $1,500-$2,000.

Pair of 16" tall candlesticks with heavy gold gilt. Underglaze factory mark in green, T&V Limoges France, Tressemann & Vogt Mark 7, ca. 1892-1907. $495-$695.

Jardinière, 8" x 11", with elephant heads as handles and separate base. Underglaze factory mark in green, W.G.&Co., Limoges France, William Guérin Mark 3, ca. 1900-1932. $1,200-$1,500.

Jardinière, 11.5" tall, with elephant heads as handles and separate base. Underglaze factory mark in green, J.P.L. France, Jean Pouyat Mark 5, ca. 1890-1932. $2,500-$3,000.

Jardinière, 11.5" tall, with lion heads as handles and separate base. Underglaze factory mark in green, D&Co., France, Délinières & Co., Mark 3, ca. 1894-1900. $2,500-$3,000.

Jardinière, 11.5" x 11" footed with handles, large pastel roses inside a reserve with a light blue green finish, highlighted with gold. Underglaze factory mark in green, T&V France, Tressemann & Vogt Mark 5a, ca. 1892-1907. $2,000-$2,500.

Jardinière, 10" x 10" with unreadable paper import mark, artist signed "H.E. Page" and dated 1897. Underglaze factory mark in green, with anchor and Limoges France, Lanternier Mark 4, ca. 1891-1914. $3,500-$4,000.

A nineteenth century mantel and original fireplace surround make this huge fireplace the center of this living room. A Victorian needlepoint fireplace screen stands in front of the opening and a large mirror is above, reflecting fabulous pieces of Sevres and Limoges porcelain.

Reverse side of jardinière, hand painted with beautiful roses.

Jardinière, 11" x 12" on separate base, artist's initials "L.M.N." and dated April 1898. Underglaze factory mark D&Co., Délinières & Co., Mark 1, ca. 1870s. $2,500-$3,000.

Jardinière, 11" x 12", includes separate base. Underglaze factory mark in green, D&Co., France, Délinières & Co., Mark 3, ca. 1894-1900. $2,500-$3,000.

Rare match holder with striker on bottom. Artist signed "M.E.B. Hutchins" dated 1907. Underglaze factory mark in green, D&Co., France, Délinières & Co., Mark 3, ca. 1894-1900. $300-$400.

Vase, 9.5" tall, underglaze factory mark in green, J.P.L. France, Jean Pouyat Mark 5, ca. 1890-1932. $900-$1,200.

Vase, 12" tall, artist signed "L.M. Cowgill." Underglaze factory mark in green, J.P.L. France, Jean Pouyat Mark 5, ca. 1890-1932. $1,600-$1,800.

Formal Victorian living room with nineteenth century settee and matching chairs upholstered in silk fabric that complement the chrysanthemums in the large Limoges jardinière on the marble top table. High ceilings allow for a large grouping of Limoges chargers hanging on the wall.

Gilt table has a rare Sevres urn, hand painted with a woman and cherubs. A pair of matching Limoges vases sit on either side of the urn and centered above it is a painting on porcelain with cherubs. The cherub and woman theme is predominant in all of these lovely pieces of art.

Vase, 14" tall, artist signed "Wirkner." Underglaze factory mark in green, J.P.L. France, Jean Pouyat Mark 5, ca. 1891-1932. $2,000-$2,500.

Vase, 14" tall, artist signed "K. Ruybix." Underglaze factory mark in green, J.P.L. France, Jean Pouyat Mark 5, ca. 1891-1932. A wonderful pair of vases hand painted by different artists. $2,000-$2,500.

Painting on porcelain, 16" x 14" in original frame, artist signed. Underglaze factory mark in green, T&V France, Tressemann & Vogt, Mark 5a, ca. 1892-1907. $3,500-$5,000.

Jardinière and base, 8" x 11.5" tall. Underglaze factory mark in green, J.P.L. France, Jean Pouyat Mark 5, ca. 1891-1932. $1,200-$2,000.

Reverse side of jardinière.

Rare jardinière, 12" x 14", with twisted handles on a fluted pedestal base. Underglaze factory mark in green, J.P.L. France, Jean Pouyat Mark 5, ca. 1890-1932. $2,400-$2,500.

Jardinière, 8" x 12", with lions' heads as handles. Underglaze factory mark in green, D&Co., Délinières & Co., Mark 1, ca. 1870s. $3,500-$4,000.

Reverse side of jardinière.

Jardinière, 8" x 12", with lions' head handles. Underglaze factory mark in green, D&Co., Délinières & Co., Mark 1, ca. 1870s. $3,500-$4,000.

Jardinière, 8" x 12", with lions' heads as handles. Underglaze factory mark in green, D&Co., Délinières & Co., Mark 1, ca. 1870s. $3,500-$4,000.

Jardinière, 10.5 " tall, with ornate handles and four gold feet. Underglaze factory mark in green, D&Co., Délinières & Co., Mark 3, ca. 1894-1900. $2,500-$3,000.

Jardinière, 8" x 12", with lions' head handles on separate base. Underglaze factory mark in green, D&Co., Délinières & Co., Mark 1, ca. 1870s. $3,500-$4,000.

Jardinière, 10.5" tall, with handles and unusual blue gray coloring with white roses. Underglaze factory mark in green, D&Co., Délinières & Co., Mark 3, ca. 1894-1900. $2,500-$3,000.

Jardinière, 11" tall, with ornate handles and pastel roses. Underglaze factory mark in green, D&Co., Délinières & Co., Mark 3, ca. 1894-1900. $2,500-$3,000.

Jardinière, 11" tall, with ornate handles and cherubs. Underglaze factory mark in green, D&Co., Délinières & Co., Mark 3, ca. $2,500-$3,000.

Left: Huge planter, 16" tall, with pastel roses. Underglaze factory mark in green, W.G.&Co., Limoges France, William Guérin Mark 3, ca. 1900-1932. $1,500-$2,000.

Right: Planter, 14" tall, with dark red, pink, and yellow roses. Underglaze factory mark in green, W.G.&Co., Limoges France, William Guérin Mark 3, ca. 1900-1932. $1,500-$2,000.

Jardinière, 8" x 12", on separate base with heavy gold gilt and matching tray. Underglaze factory mark in green, D&Co., Délinières & Co., Mark 1, ca. 1870s. Set $3,000-$3,500.

Charger, 14" diameter, artist signed "E. Miler." Underglaze factory mark in green, T&V Limoges France, Tressemann & Vogt Mark 7, ca. 1892-1907. $800-$1,200.

Charger, 14" diameter. Underglaze mark in green W.G.&Co., William Guérin Mark 2, ca. 1891-1900. $600-$800.

Charger, 14" diameter. Underglaze factory mark in green, Haviland France, Mark I, ca. 1894-1931. $700-$800.

Charger, 12" diameter. Underglaze factory mark in green, D&Co., Délinières & Co., Mark 3, ca. 1894-1900. $400-$600.

Tray, 18" diameter. Underglaze factory mark in green, T&V Limoges France, Tressemann & Vogt Mark 7, ca. 1892-1907. $800-$1,200.

Tray, 12" diameter. Underglaze factory mark in green, D&Co., Délinières & Co., Mark 3, ca. 1894-1900. $500-$600.

Tray, 18" diameter. Underglaze factory mark in green, GDA France, Gérard, Dufraisseix, Abbot Mark 1, ca. 1900-1941. $800-$1,200.

Opposite page, left: Lovely nineteenth century hand painted French vitrine outlined with ormolu houses a fabulous collection of unusual Limoges.

Chop tray, 16" diameter. Underglaze factory mark in green, T&V Limoges France, Tressemann & Vogt Mark 7, ca. 1892-1907. $600-$700.

Tray, 16" diameter. Underglaze factory mark in green, T&V Limoges France, Tressemann & Vogt Mark 7, ca. 1892-1907. $600-$800.

Tray, 16" diameter. Underglaze factory mark in green, T&V Limoges France, Tressemann & Vogt, Mark 7, ca. 1892-1907. $600-$800.

Tray, 18" diameter. Underglaze factory mark in green, D&Co., Délinières & Co., Mark 3, ca. 1894-1900. $800-$1,200.

Unusual vase, 8" x 13.5", painted in Art Nouveau style, artist signed "Vera Gray." Underglaze factory mark in green, T&V Limoges France, Tressemann & Vogt Mark 7, ca. 1892-1907. This vase has been in various Limoges reference books since the 1980s with the value increasing from $300 to the current value of $2,000.

Vase, 6" x 9", painted in lovely shades of blue with roses. Underglaze factory mark in green, T&V Limoges France, Tressemann & Vogt Mark 7, ca 1892-1907. $600-$800.

Vase, 11.5" tall, with reticulated border. Underglaze factory mark in green, B&Co., Bernardaud & Co., Mark 1, ca. $750-$800.

Vase, 12" tall, artist signed "A. Hall" and dated 1907. Underglaze factory mark in green, J.P.L. France, Jean Pouyat Mark 5, ca. 1890-1932. $1,000-$1,200.

Vase, 14" tall, with ornate handles, signed in gold on bottom "Hand Painted Through Out." Overglaze decorating mark in red, Elite Limoges France, Bawo & Dotter Mark 8, ca. 1896-1900. $2,000-$2,500.

Plaque, 13.25" tall x 9.25 wide, rare blank. Underglaze factory mark in green, Limoges in star, Coiffe Mark 1, ca. before 1890. $600-$800.

Plaque, 13.25 tall x 9.25 wide. Underglaze factory mark in green, Limoges in star, Coiffe Mark 1, ca. before 1890. $600-$800.

This fireplace is in a nineteenth century, Gothic Revival style Victorian home that has remained in the same family for four generations. The mantel is made of Vermont slate and faux painted with a dipping process using oil and water. Handsome hand painted gold trim accents the slate. The fireplace is lined with iron for coal burning. Hanging above the mantel is an 1879 pre-Raphaelite print of "The Dreamers," by artist Albert Moore. Complementing the print are Limoges vases and a tea set.

Vase, 13.5" tall. Underglaze factory mark in green, PL Limoges France, LA Porcelaine Limousine Mark, 1 ca. 1905-1930. $1,200-$1,500.

Large vase, 20" tall, artist signed "E. Miler." Unmarked, but attributed to the Limoges factories. $1,500-2,000.

Tea set, hand painted with roses and cherubs, artist's initials "MY" and dated 1904. Underglaze factory mark in green, J.P.L. France, Jean Pouyat Mark 5, ca. 1890-1932. $700-$900.

Ebonized, Louis XVI style, ormolu-mounted writing desk inset with two Limoges plaques. In the late eighteenth century, it was fashionable to have porcelain inlaid on the tops or sides of tables or inset into doors. This desk, from the early 1900s, was fashioned after such superb period pieces of furniture.

Hand painted oval pieces of porcelain, 10" x 6", inset into the doors of the writing desk. Each inset depicts a man and a woman in a traditional eighteenth century courting scene. Both are signed with an illegible artist's signature.

Plaque, 14" diameter, artist signed "Muville." Overglaze decorating mark in red, crown with initials, L.R.&L., Lazeyras, Rosenfeld & Lehman Mark 2, ca. 1920s. $1,600-$1,800.

Plaque, 14" diameter, artist signed "Muville." Overglaze decorating mark in gray with crown and initials L.R.&L., Lazeyras, Rosenfeld & Lehman Mark 3, ca. 1920s. $1,600-$1,800.

Top left: Plaque, 14" diameter, artist signed "Muville." Overglaze decorating mark in red, crown with initials, L.R.&L., Lazeyras, Rosenfeld & Lehman Mark 2, ca. 1920s. $1,600-$1,800.

Bottom left: Plaque, 14" diameter, hand painted with a bare breasted maiden. Overglaze decorating mark in green, torch with Limoges France, Flambeau China Mark 4, ca. 1890s-1900s. $800-$1,200.

Top right: Charger, 14" diameter, artist signed "Dubois." Overglaze decorating mark, Limoges France in an oval shape, Limoges France Mark 8, ca. after 1891. $1,400-$1,600.

Bottom right: Charger, 13.5" diameter, artist signed "Dubois." Underglaze factory mark in green, AK France, Klingenberg Mark 7, ca. 1890s-1910. $800-$1,200.

Charger, 12.5" diameter, artist signed "Lancy." Overglaze decorating mark in red, crown with Porcelaine Limoges France, Lazeyras, Rosenfeld & Lehman Mark 2, ca. 1920s. $800-$1000.

Charger, 18" diameter, artist signed "Dubois." Overglaze decorating mark in red, torch with Limoges France, Flambeau Mark 2, ca. 1890s. $1,800-$2,000.

Charger, 13" diameter, illegible artist's signature. Overglaze decorating mark in gray with crown, Lazeyras, Rosenfeld & Lehman Mark 3, ca. 1920s. $800-$1,000.

Charger, 13" diameter. Overglaze mark in red, crown with initials, L.R.&L., Lazeyras, Rosenfeld & Lehman Mark 2, ca. 1920s. $500-$600.

This cape home with a beamed ceiling living room looks elegant with Limoges hand painted plates used as a border. Special pieces accessorize the room and complement a collection in the adjacent dining room.

Lamp, 16" tall, bulbous with a fantastic portrait of a woman and two children. Underglaze factory mark in green, J.P.L. France, Jean Pouyat Mark 5, ca. 1891-1932. $1,500-$2,000.

Bottom left: A massed collection of floral chargers and trays frames a lovely piece of art on canvas. All of the colors complement the dyes used in the needlepoint rug.

Serving tray with handles, 15.5" diameter. Underglaze factory mark in green, T&V Limoges, Tressemann & Vogt Mark 4b, ca. 1892-1907. $600-$800.

Bowl, 12" diameter, on four feet. Underglaze factory mark in green, T&V Limoges France, Tressemann & Vogt Mark 7, ca. 1892-1907. $395-$495.

Elongated celery tray, 16" in length, artist signed "Duval." Underglaze factory mark in green, J.P.L. France, Jean Pouyat Mark 5, ca. 1890-1932. Overglaze decorating mark, Jean Pouyat Mark 8, ca. 1906-1932. $295-$395.

Plate, 12.5" diameter. Underglaze factory mark in green, T&V Limoges, Tressemann & Vogt Mark 4b, ca. 1892-1907. $700-$900.

Bowl, 8" diameter, on four feet. Underglaze factory mark in green, T&V Limoges France, Tressemann & Vogt Mark 7, ca. 1892-1907. $295-$395.

Charger or flat tray, 13" diameter. Underglaze factory mark in green, J.P.L. France, Jean Pouyat Mark 5, ca. 1891-1932. $800-$1,000.

Charger, 12.5" diameter, with scalloped edge. Underglaze factory mark in green, AK France, Klingenberg Mark 7, ca. 1890s-1910. $800-$1,000

Tray with edge, 13" diameter. Underglaze factory mark in green, T&V Limoges France Déposé, Tressemann & Vogt Mark 8, ca. 1907-1919. $900-$1,200

Charger, 12.5" diameter, with scalloped edge. Underglaze factory mark in green, T&V Limoges France, Tressemann & Vogt Mark 7, ca. 1892-1907. $900-$1,200.

Charger, 12" diameter, with scalloped edge. Underglaze factory mark in green, AK France, Klingenberg Mark 7, ca. 1890s-1910. $800-$1,000

Charger or flat tray, 12.5" diameter. Underglaze factory mark in green, T&V Limoges France, Tressemann & Vogt Mark 7, ca. 1892-1907. $475-$600.

Charger or flat tray, 12.5" diameter. Underglaze factory mark in green, T&V Limoges France, Tressemann & Vogt Mark 7, ca. 1892-1907. $475-$600.

Dessert plate, 9.5" diameter. Underglaze factory mark in green, J.P.L. France, Jean Pouyat Mark 5, ca. 1891-1932. $70-$100.

Dessert plate, 10" diameter. Underglaze factory mark in green, T&V Limoges, Tressemann & Vogt Mark 4b, ca. 1892-1907. $70-$100.

Dessert plate, 9.5" diameter. Underglaze factory mark in green, Haviland France, Mark I, ca. 1894-1931. $90-$100.

Dessert plate, 10" diameter. Underglaze factory mark in green, T&V Limoges France, Tressemann & Vogt Mark 7, ca. 1892-1907. $75-$95.

Dessert plate, 9.5" diameter. Underglaze factory mark in green, Haviland France, Mark I, ca. 1894-1931. $200-$250.

Dessert plate, 10" diameter. Underglaze factory mark in green, W.G.&Co., Limoges France, William Guérin Mark 3, ca. 1900-1932. $90-$100.

Dessert plate, 9.75" diameter, artist's initials "R.L." and dated 1900. Underglaze factory mark in green, J.P.L. France, Jean Pouyat Mark 5, ca. 1891-1932. $90-$145.

Dessert plate, 10" diameter. Underglaze factory mark in green, T&V France, Tressemann & Vogt Mark 5a, ca. 1892-1907. $90-$100.

Dessert plate, 9.75" diameter, artist's initials "R.L." and dated 1900. Underglaze factory mark in green J.P.L. France, Jean Pouyat Mark 5, ca. 1891-1932. $90-$145.

Dessert plate, 8" diameter, one from a set of twelve. Underglaze factory mark in green, J.P.L. France, Jean Pouyat Mark 5, ca. 1891-1932. Set $495-$695.

Dessert plate, 9" diameter, with gold edge. Underglaze factory mark in green, J.P.L. France, Jean Pouyat Mark 5, ca. 1891-1932. Overglaze decorating mark with green and pink wreath, Jean Pouyat Mark 9, ca. after 1914-1932. $150-$175.

Dessert plate, 10.5" diameter, with heavy etched gold gilt rim. Underglaze factory mark in green, J.P.L. France, Jean Pouyat Mark 5, ca. 1891-1932. Overglaze decorating mark with green and pink wreath, Jean Pouyat Mark 9, ca. after 1914-1932. $200-$225.

A beamed living room ceiling is made elegant with an oval mirror in a gilt frame surrounded by five lovely large chargers. Reflected in the mirror is a collection of doorstops on the mantel.

Charger, 13" diameter, with heavy gold. Underglaze factory mark in green, D&Co., France, Délinières & Co., Mark 3, ca. 1894-1900. $1,000-$1,200.

Charger, 12.5" diameter. Underglaze factory mark in green, J.P.L. France, Jean Pouyat Mark 5, ca. 1890-1932. $800-$1,200.

Charger, 12.5" diameter. Underglaze factory mark in green, T&V France, Tressemann & Vogt, Mark 5a, ca. 1892-1907. $700-$900.

Charger, 12.5" diameter. Underglaze factory mark in green, T&V France, Tressemann & Vogt Mark 5a, ca. 1892-1907. $800-$1,200.

Charger, 12.5" diameter. Underglaze factory mark in green, T&V Limoges France, Tressemann & Vogt Mark 7, ca. 1892-1907. $800-$1,200.

An elegant living room with tables featuring small collections of Limoges: frames, tea sets, and vases.

Large squat vase, 16" diameter, with hand painted chrysanthemums. Underglaze factory mark in green, T&V Limoges France, Tressemann & Vogt Mark 7, ca. 1892-1907. $1,500-$2,000.

This dramatic wall covering is the perfect canvas for a grouping of two Limoges chargers and a Limoges cake plate.

Large planter or jardinière in the shape of a champagne bucket, 9.5" tall. Underglaze factory mark in green, B&Co., Bernardaud & Co., Mark 1, ca. 1900-1914. $1,000-$1,500.

A living room accessorized with a Limoges lamp, a collection of vases, and a large punch bowl as the focal point on the coffee table. The floral theme is repeated in the fabric used to upholster the couch and matching pillows.

This fireplace would be the focal point of the living room, if not for the lovely collection of Limoges used on the mantel and on the wall above. A large ice cream platter and eight matching serving bowls complement the shape of the large round stones from a local quarry used in this fireplace surround.

Large Limoges punch bowl, 13.5" diameter on separate base. Underglaze factory mark in green, T&V Limoges France, Tressemann & Vogt, Mark 7, ca. 1892-1907. Overglaze mark in red, HANDPAINTED PICARD CHINA. $3,500-$4,500.

Punch bowl, 13.5" diameter, hand painted with grapes. Underglaze factory mark in green, Limoges France with three stars, Plainemaison Mark 1, ca. 1890s-1910. $2,000-$2,500.

Small punch bowl hand painted with apples. Underglaze factory mark in green, T&V Limoges France Déposé, Tressemann & Vogt Mark 8, ca. 1907-1919. $800-$1,300.

Punch bowl with hand painted roses. Underglaze factory mark in green, T&V Limoges France Déposé, Tressemann & Vogt Mark 8, ca. 1907-1919. $2,000-$2,500.

Vase, 13.3" tall, with gold ornate twisted handles. Underglaze factory mark in green, Latrille Frères Mark 1, ca. 1899-1913. $700-$1,200.

Vase, 10.5" tall, with ornate dragon handles. Underglaze factory mark in green, J.P.L. France, Jean Pouyat Mark 5, ca. 1890-1932. $800-$1,000.

Reserve of vase.

Vase, 5.75" tall, with heavy gold on rim. Underglaze factory mark in green, J.P.L. France, Jean Pouyat Mark 5, ca. 1890-1932. $225-$250.

Large vase, 14.5" tall. Underglaze factory mark in green, H. Balleroy Mark 1, ca. 1908-1930s. $900-$1,200.

Vase, 12" tall. Underglaze factory mark in green, D&Co., France, Délinières & Co., Mark 3, ca. 1894-1900. $800-$1,000.

Left: Muscle vase, 12" tall, with double handles. Underglaze factory mark in green, J.P.L. France, Jean Pouyat Mark 5, ca. 1890-1932. $700-$800.

Right: Vase, 7.5" tall with double handles. Underglaze factory mark in green, J.P.L. France, Jean Pouyat Mark 5, ca. 1890-1932. $300-$400.

The Dining Room

A beautiful dining room showcases this massive collection. The 1920s dining room table with red velvet tablecloth dramatically displays a white and gold dinnerware set.

Furnish the dining room as you would any other room and create new possibilities for displaying a Limoges collection. French vitrines, Oriental tables, sideboards, and hand painted plant stands make a dramatic stage for a Limoges collection. A piece of Limoges can transform a room. An entire collection creates a beautifully balanced, elegant, yet relaxed and welcoming room. Grouping together similar pieces will create an appealing still life.

Emphasize the unusualness of a fireplace in a dining room. Overhang the mantel with assorted Limoges pieces appropriate for the table. Accessorize your mantel with Limoges pitchers, goblets, platters, and plates. The fireplace surround can be painted with trompe l'oeil to replicate a scene on a favorite piece of Limoges.

Simplicity often means drama and a single Limoges punch bowl or jardinière can make a dining table elegant. A Limoges vase used as a centerpiece embraces the Limoges dinnerware at each place setting and extends the floral theme.

The focal point of this room is definitely the set dining room table. Combining different Limoges dinnerware patterns on the same table creates a table with a singularly dramatic sense of style. With gilt Limoges dinner plates, just a few accoutrements are needed to dress the table for a formal occasion. Integrating pieces of sterling and glass make an elegant, inviting dinner table and account for an appealing informal balance.

Showcasing a family's beloved Wedding Band porcelain (see next section) in a china cabinet, on a wall, or on a table makes an elegant yet inexpensive art collage. Displaying a Limoges collection brings individuality to a dining room and adds a personal touch.

A Limoges punch bowl with large white peonies serves as a stunning centerpiece and complements the drama of large brass candelabras.

Twelve dinnerware plates, 12" with thick gold rim. Underglaze factory mark in green, W.G.&Co., Limoges France, William Guérin Company Mark 3, ca. 1900-1932. Set of twelve $1,200-$1,500.

The top of this ornate gold china cabinet is perfect for a fabulous display of roses so vibrant and colorful you'd think you were in a garden. Vase with gold handles is unmarked, other pieces wear the underglaze factory marks from the William Guérin Factory and Tressemann & Vogt Factory.

Dinnerware set for twelve, 12" dinner plates, 8.5" dessert or salad plates with raised gold embossing on the edges. Underglaze mark in green, Haviland France, Mark I, ca. 1894-1931. Set of twelve $2,000-$2,200.

Modern dining room is perfect for large, dramatic pieces of Limoges. A single bowl in the center of the table adds drama to the room.

A Limoges grouping on a sideboard mixed with a Waterford candelabra makes the perfect still life.

Punch bowl, 10" x 14", with etched heavy gold on separate base and twelve matching punch cups. Underglaze factory mark in green, D&Co France, Délinières & Co. Mark 3 with "White's Art Co. Chicago Hand Painted" decorating mark, ca. 1914-1923. $3,000-$3,500.

Fabulous oval tray, 18" with rare subject matter, a scene from Othello encircled by heavy and ornate gold gilt raised paint and enameling. Underglaze factory mark in green, T&V Limoges France Depose, Tressemann & Vogt Mark 8, ca. 1907-1919. $2,000-$3,000.

Large vase, 16" with etched heavy gold, artist signed "Laura H. Haste" and dated 1922. Underglaze factory mark in green, B&C France, Bernardaud & Co. Mark 1, ca. 1900-1914. $1,000-$1,500.

Pair of candlesticks, 7.5" tall, in solid gold. Underglaze factory mark in green, W.G. Limoges France, William Guérin Mark 3, ca. 1900-1932. $295-$395.

Unusual 18" punch bowl with attached pedestal holds a large house plant, making a dramatic statement against the white wall. Large painting on porcelain is mixed with Sevres and KPM pieces.

Large dining room with punch bowl in the center of the table. A vase on the corner vitrine and a tankard with matching set of mugs on a lovely Bombay chest accessorize this dining room to perfection.

Excellent example of vernacular Queen Anne dining room in the E. Sibbill Banks House, Waltham, Massachusetts, National Register of Historic Places.

Mixing sterling, crystal, vaseline glass, and porcelain creates an elegant table top. No detail is overlooked, from the Limoges salts and sterling salt spoons to the French porcelain place card holders.

Top right: Various sets of Limoges dinnerware are used to create a one of a kind, unique place setting.

Bottom right: Dinner plate, 11.5" diameter. Underglaze factory mark in green, J.P.L. France, Jean Pouyat Mark 5, ca. 1914-1932. Overglaze decorating mark with green and pink wreath, Jean Pouyat Mark 9, ca. after 1914-1932. Set of eight $800-$1,200.

Limoges vase, 13" tall. Underglaze factory mark in green, PL Limoges France, La Porcelaine Limousine Mark 1, ca. 1905-late 1930s. $900-$1,200.

Dessert plate, 9" diameter. Underglaze factory mark in green, J.P.L France, Jean Pouyat Mark 5, ca. 1914-1932. Overglaze decorating mark with green and pink wreath, Jean Pouyat Mark 9, ca. after 1914-1932. Set of eight $400-$500.

Dinner plate, 11.5" diameter. Underglaze factory mark in green, H&Co., L France, Mark H, ca. 1888-1896. $125-$175 each. Matching cup and saucer, underglaze factory mark in green, Haviland & Company Marks I, ca. 1894-1931. $75-$95 each.

Five piece dinnerware set for twelve includes: dinner plate, 11.5"; dessert plate, 8.5"; salad plate, 6"; bowl, 5.5" diameter; cup, 3.5" tall; and saucer, 5" diameter. Underglaze factory mark, H&Co., L France, Mark H., ca. 1888-1896. Set of twelve $3,500-$4,500.

One from a set of eight dinner plates, 12" diameter, artist signed "Blanche Miller McFeely" and in wreath, "Elizabeth." Underglaze factory mark in green, T&V Limoges France Déposé, Tressemann & Vogt Mark 8, ca. 1907-1919. Set $1,500-$2,000.

One from a set of eight dinner plates, 11.5" diameter, heavy gold gilt on front and back rim. Underglaze factory mark in green, W.G.&Co., Limoges France, William Guérin Mark 3, ca. after 1900-1932. Set $800-$1,200.

Another from the of set of eight above, each uniquely hand painted.

One from a set of eight dinner plates, 12" diameter. Underglaze factory mark in green, T&V Limoges France, Déposé, Tressemann & Vogt Mark 8, ca. 1907-1919. Set $400-$800.

One from a set of twelve dinner plates, 11.5" diameter, with matching cup, 2.5" tall, and saucer, 5" diameter. Underglaze factory mark in green, GDA France, Gérard, Dufraisseix, and Abbot, Mark 1, ca. 1900-1941. Overglaze decorating mark in red, Gérard, Dufraisseix, and Abbot, Mark 3, ca. 1900-1941. Set $1,800-$2,000.

One from a set of six dinner plates, 11.5 diameter, with matching cup, 2.5" tall, and saucer, 5" diameter. Hand painted gold on rim impressed with fruit. Underglaze factory mark in green, W.G.&Co., Limoges France, William Guérin Mark 3, ca. after 1900-1932. Set $600-$800.

Matching dinner plate.

Set of four unique dinner plates, 10.5" diameter. Underglaze factory mark in green, J.P.L. France, Jean Pouyat Mark 5, ca. 1891-1932. Overglaze decorating mark with green and pink wreath, Jean Pouyat Mark 9, ca. 1914-1932. Set $400-$500.

Matching dinner plate.

Matching dinner plate.

Dinner plate, 11.5" diameter. Underglaze factory mark in green, J.P.L. France, Jean Pouyat Mark 5, ca. 1891-1932. Overglaze decorating mark with green and pink wreath, Jean Pouyat Mark 9, ca. 1914-1932. $25-$75 each.

Dinner plate, 11.5" diameter. Underglaze factory mark in green, J.P.L. France, Jean Pouyat Mark 5, ca. 1891-1932. Overglaze decorating mark with green and pink wreath, Jean Pouyat Mark 9, ca. 1914-1932. $25-$75 each.

Dinner plate, 11.5" diameter. Underglaze factory mark in green, J.P.L. France, Jean Pouyat Mark 5, ca. 1891-1932. Overglaze decorating mark with green and pink wreath, Jean Pouyat Mark 9, ca. 1914-1932. $25-$75 each.

Dinner plate, 11.5" diameter. Underglaze factory mark in green, J.P.L. France, Jean Pouyat Mark 5, ca. 1891-1932. Overglaze decorating mark with green and pink wreath, Jean Pouyat Mark 9, ca. 1914-1932. $25-$75 each.

Dinner plate, 12" diameter. Underglaze factory mark in green, J.P.L. France, Jean Pouyat Mark 5, ca. 1891-1932. Overglaze decorating mark with green and pink wreath, Jean Pouyat Mark 9, ca. 1914-1932.

Ornate Victorian oak sideboard is the perfect display cabinet for a varied porcelain collection.

Set of five piece dinnerware for twelve includes: dinner plate, 11.5"; dessert plate, 8.5"; salad plate, 6"; bowl, 5.5" diameter; cup, 3.5" tall; and saucer, 5" diameter. Impressed initials "T&H" and overglaze decorating mark in red, Theodore Haviland Mark r, ca. 1925. Set $595-$795.

The floral design of this 13" tall Limoges vase and 12" diameter chop tray blend perfectly with the wallpaper and the applied carving on the sideboard.

Large dining areas with high ceilings are conducive to massive pieces of nineteenth century Victorian furniture that hold collections of various shapes and sizes.

Natural wood door frames have corner blocks with medallions in beautiful detail. Charger, 13.5" diameter has artist's signature "ELC" and is dated 1893. Underglaze factory mark in green, H&Co., Limoges France Mark H, ca. 1888-1896. $295-$395.

Tops of furniture make great shelves for large pieces of Limoges .

Fruit bowl, 12" diameter. Underglaze factory mark in green, J.P.L. France, Jean Pouyat Mark 5, ca. 1891-1932. Overglaze decorating mark with green and pink wreath, Jean Pouyat Mark 9, ca. after 1914-1932. $80-$120.

Celery dish, 11.5". Underglaze factory mark in green, J.P.L. France, Jean Pouyat Mark 5, ca. 1891-1932. Overglaze decorating mark with green and pink wreath, Jean Pouyat Mark 9, ca. after 1914-1932. $35-$75.

Punch bowl on matching base, 13.5" x 8.5", artist's initials "RV" on outside of the bowl. Underglaze factory mark in green, T&V Limoges France, Tressemann & Vogt Mark 7, ca. 1892-1907. Overglaze decorating mark in purple, with script "Hand Painted" T&V Limoges in bell, Tressemann & Vogt Mark 16b, ca. 1907-1919. $2,200-$2,500.

Serving bowl on feet, 5.5" diameter. Underglaze factory mark in green, Elite L/France, Bawo & Dotter Mark 5, ca. after 1900. Overglaze mark in red, "Higgins & Seiter NY." $55-$75.

Platter, 18", artist signed on front "Dubois" with unusual purple colors and pheasant. Underglaze factory mark in green, star with France, Coiffe Mark 2, ca. 1891-1914. $2,000-$2,200.

Platter, 16.5", with thick gold rim and hand painted roses as a center medallion. Underglaze factory mark in green, Vignaud Limoges, Vignaud Frères Mark 1, ca. 1911-1938. $395-$495.

Large serving tray, 18", hand painted with roses. Underglaze factory mark in green, H&Co underscored with L, Mark F, ca. 1876-1889. $900-$1,000.

Massive oval tray, 22" diameter. Underglaze factory mark in green, T&V Limoges France, Tressemann & Vogt Mark 7, ca. 1892-1907. $400-$600.

Elegant and dramatic nineteenth century Vermont slate fireplace with etched gold is dramatic against this red wall. Only one of the many focal points in this large room with high ceilings, the pieces on the mantel are large, elegant, and simple.

Painting on porcelain, 18" diameter, artist's initials "E.L.C." Underglaze factory mark in green, T&V France, Mark 5a, ca. 1892-1907. $2,500-$3,500.

Hand painted ceiling is one of the many details that has not been overlooked in this Victorian dining room. An inherited punch bowl and a cider set with fruit plaque are on the massive table.

Fabulous nineteenth century gold gilt cabinet with hand painted inserts houses a wonderful collection of jardinières, ferners, planters, and vase.

Punch bowl, 12" diameter, has dramatic hand-painting with raised gold, no markings. $800-$900.

Ferner, 5" x 8", with hand painted cameo panels of roses. Underglaze factory mark in green, Limoges France, Mark 6, ca. after 1891. $550-$700.

Ferner, 5.5" x 7", beautiful hand painted violets. Underglaze factory mark in green, D & C with one line and then France, Délinières & Co., Mark 3, ca. 1894-1900. $550-$700.

Ferner, 5.5" x 9", entire piece hand painted with roses including the bottom (not shown). Underglaze factory mark in green, D & C with one line and France, Délinières & Co., Mark 3, ca. 1894-1900. $700-$1,200.

Ferner, 5.5" x 7", fabulous hand painted roses with heavily gilded feet. Overglaze decorating mark in green with Coronet, Borgfeldt, Mark 1, ca. 1906-1920. $550-$700.

Jardinière, 5.5" x 9.5", with deeply scalloped four footed base and griffin-shaped handles, looking like swans. Unmarked blank attributed to the d' Albis and Romanet Factory, ca. 1896. $800-$1,200.

Jardinière, 9" x 9.5", with gilded handles and feet. Underglaze factory mark in green, D&Co., France, Délinières & Co., Mark 3, ca. 1894-1900. $1,500-$2,000.

Jardinière, 8" x 10", blank attributed to the d' Albis and Romanet Factory, ca. 1896. Hand painted, factory overglaze mark in red with Elite Works, without Bawo & Dotter, Mark 9a, ca. 1900-1914. $1,000-$1,400.

Jardinière, 8" x 10", blank attributed to the d' Albis and Romanet Factory, ca. 1896. Hand painted, factory overglaze mark in red with Elite Works, without Bawo & Dotter, Mark 9a, ca. 1900-1914. $1,000-$1,400.

Jardinière, 12" x 14" tall, including the separate base height. Gold gilt hand painted lions' head handles and paw feet, with roses all around. Underglaze factory mark in green, D&C France, Délinières & Co., Mark 3, ca. 1894-1900. $3,500-$4,500.

Unique ferner or planter, 8" x 12.5" in length, hand painted with vibrant multi-colored chrysanthemums, gold gilt handles and four feet. Underglaze factory mark in green, D&Co., France, Délinières & Co., Mark 3, ca. 1894-1900. $1,500-$2,500.

Reverse of jardinière.

Vase, 11" tall, with serpent handles hand painted by the same artist who decorated the unique ferner. Underglaze factory mark in green, J.P.L. France, Jean Pouyat Mark 5, ca. 1890-1932. $750-$950.

Ferner, 4.5" x 9", hand painted, factory decorated piece. Underglaze factory mark in green, T & V initials with Limoges France, Tressemann & Vogt Mark 7, ca. 1892-1907, probably latter part of period. Overglaze mark in purple with Limoges printed above bell and accompanied with a banner printed Hand Painted, ca. 1907-1919. Piece dates 1907. $600-$700.

Ferner, 8.5" diameter. Underglaze factory mark in green, AK France, Klingenberg & Dwenger Mark 7, ca. 1890s-1910. $400-$500.

Cider set has a pitcher with six matching mugs. All pieces in the set have the underglaze factory mark in green, J.P.L. France, Jean Pouyat Mark 5, ca. 1890-1932. Set $1,200-$1,600.

Cider pitcher, 10.5" from lip to handle, artist signed "Roby." Underglaze factory mark, T&V France, Tressemann & Vogt Mark 5a, ca. 1892-1907. Overglaze decorating mark in purple, Tressemann & Vogt Mark 15. $650-1,000.

Pitcher, 9" x 8", heavy gold with enameling, artist signed "Worth." Underglaze mark in green, Haviland France, Haviland Mark I, ca. 1894-1931. $650-$1,000.

Reverse of cider pitcher.

Cider pitcher, 9", artist signed "B. Young Shook." Underglaze factory mark in green, J.P.L. France, Jean Pouyat Mark 5, ca. 1891-1932. $450-$550.

Cider pitcher, 9", with lovely apples. Underglaze factory mark in green, J.P.L. France, Jean Pouyat Mark 5, ca. 1891-1932. $550-$650.

Cider pitcher, 9.5", with hand painted purple background and lovely pink roses. Underglaze factory mark in green, T&V Limoges France, Tressemann & Vogt Mark 7, ca. 1892-1907. Overglaze decorating mark in purple, Tressemann & Vogt Mark 15. $495-$595.

Cider pitcher, 7", artist signed "E. Miler." Underglaze factory mark in green, J.P.L. France, Jean Pouyat Mark 5, ca. 1891-1932. $450-$550.

Cider pitcher, 9", with hand painted roses. Underglaze factory mark in green, J.P.L. France, Jean Pouyat Mark 5, ca. 1891-1932. $450-$550.

Grand dining takes place in this large dining room with high ceilings, ceiling medallion, and unique antique chandelier with twelve arms. Period furniture and large French vitrines are perfect for large collections of Limoges.

Chocolate pot, 10" tall, with beautiful hand painted scene in heavy raised gold outline. Underglaze factory mark in green, T&V Limoges, Tressemann & Vogt Mark 4b, ca. 1892-1907. $450-$850.

Beautiful Limoges dinnerware in red and crimson along with crystal stemware makes for elegant and formal dining.

Bouillon cup and saucer, 2" tall, with ornate raised gold gilt and hand painted roses. Artist's initials "LPL" and dated 1905. Underglaze factory mark, Haviland & Co., Mark I. $75-$195.

Twelve place dinnerware set in red and gold includes 12" dinner plate, 9" salad or dessert plate, cup and saucer. Underglaze factory mark in green, GDA France, Gérard, Dufraisseix, and Abbot Mark 1, ca. 1900-1941. Overglaze decorating mark in red, Gérard, Dufraisseix, and Abbot Mark 3, ca. 1900-1941. Set $2,000-$2,500.

Cake plate, 11.5" diameter, and twelve matching dessert plates, 8" diameter, red and gold. Underglaze factory mark in green, Limoges France, Limoges Castel Mark, ca. 1955-1979. Set $400-$600.

Dessert plate, 9" diameter, red with gold center medallion. Underglaze factory mark in green, GDA France, Gérard, Dufraisseix, and Abbot Mark 1, ca. 1900-1941. Overglaze decorating mark in red, Gérard, Dufraisseix, and Abbot. $80-$90.

The muted and pastel colors of the accessories in this room are perfect for enhancing the needlepoint rug, handmade by the Needlepoint Club of America.

Jardinière on separate stand, 11.5" tall. Underglaze factory mark in green, D&Co., France, Délinières & Co., Mark 3, ca. 1894-1900. $2,500-$3,500.

A china cabinet's marble top is perfect for this Limoges grouping. The jardinière serves as a wonderful container for this exotic floral arrangement provided by Holland's Flowers, North Andover, Massachusetts.

Unusually massive painting on porcelain, 32" diameter in original gold frame, artist signed "E. McIveny" and dated 1902. Underglaze factory mark in green, T&V Limoges, Tressemann & Vogt Mark 4b, ca. 1892-1907. $3,000-$5,000.

Tray, 16" diameter, artist's initials "E.D.S." and dated 1913. Underglaze factory mark, T&V Limoges France, Tressemann & Vogt Mark 7, ca. 1892-1907. $600-$800.

Jardinière, 9" tall. Underglaze factory mark in green, T&V Limoges France, Tressemann & Vogt Mark 7, ca. 1892-1907. $800-$1,200

This working fireplace, in a Victorian dining room, has been painted with a trompe l'oeil scene to enhance the Limoges porcelain in the room. A romantic nineteenth century French couple in a courtyard was inserted to replicate a chocolate pot in one of the vitrines nearby and to complement the Limoges clock perched on the mantel.

A brilliant grouping of porcelains provides a kind of elegant informal balance on this mantel.

Overhanging the mantel is a large, ornate, nineteenth century mirror with a hand painted scene on the canvas insert framed above the actual mirror. The romantic theme with men and women courting is consistent in the mirror, Limoges mantel clock, and Paris Porcelain vases.

Mantel clock, 14" tall, with ornate eighteenth century scene, illegible artist's signature. Underglaze mark in green with "Made in France, Limoges" above star, the word "France" under the star, Coiffe Mark 4, ca. 1914-1920s. $1,500-$2,000.

Mantel clock, 20" tall, very ornate with dripping gold and hand painted eighteenth century figural scene insert. Overglaze mark, Elite Limoges in red, Bawo & Dotter, Mark 6, ca. 1880s-1891. $5,000-$7,000 with matching candlesticks.

Mantel clock, 12" tall, ornate with cherub scene, artist signed "Quentin." Underglaze "Made in France, Limoges" above star, the word "France" under the star, Coiffe Mark 4, ca. 1914-1920s. $1,500-$2,000.

Hanging clock, 12" diameter, hand painted. Marked "France" under the glaze, ca. 1880-1900s. $1,500-$2,000.

A china cabinet chock full of Limoges tea and chocolate sets, hand painted dinnerware, and serving pieces.

Chocolate set, consisting of chocolate pot, 12" tall, with matching sugar, creamer, and tray. Underglaze factory mark in green, J.P.L. France, Jean Pouyat Mark 5, ca. 1891-1932. Set $1,000-$1,500.

Matching cup and saucer from the chocolate set below.

Chocolate set, consisting of chocolate pot, 12.5" tall, five cups and saucers, and 14" oval tray. Underglaze factory mark in green, J.P.L. France, Jean Pouyat Mark 5, ca. 1891-1932. Set $2,000-$3,000.

Chocolate set, consisting of chocolate pot, 12" tall, and cups, 3" tall. Underglaze factory mark in green, J.P.L. France, Jean Pouyat Mark 5, ca. 1891-1932. Set $1,000-$1,500.

Matching cup and saucer. Underglaze factory mark in green, T&V Limoges France, Tressemann & Vogt Mark 7, ca. 1892-1907.

Matching tray, 12" diameter. Underglaze factory mark in green, T&V Limoges, Tressemann & Vogt Mark 4b, ca. 1892-1907. $300-$400.

Matching cup and saucer for set at left, 3" tall, artist signed "Magne." Underglaze factory mark in green, T&V Limoges France, Tressemann & Vogt Marks 7 and 11 with "All Over Hand Painted" printed with a banner in red, ca. 1892-1907.

Chocolate set, consisting of chocolate pot, 10.5" tall, six cups and saucers, and tray. Factory hand painted and artist signed "Magne" on each piece. Underglaze factory mark in green, T&V Limoges France, Tressemann & Vogt Marks 7 and 11 with "All Over Hand Painted" printed with a banner in red, ca. 1892-1907. Set $2,500-$3,000.

Chocolate pot, 11" tall, with roses. Underglaze factory mark in green, W.G.&Co., Limoges France, William Guérin Mark 3, ca. 1900-1932. $400-$600.

Matching tray for set above, 16" diameter, artist signed "Magne." Underglaze factory mark in green, T&V Limoges France, Tressemann & Vogt Marks 7 and 11 with "All Over Hand Painted" printed with a banner in red, ca. 1892-1907.

Chocolate pot, 10" tall, with roses. Underglaze factory mark in green, J.P.L. France, Jean Pouyat Mark 5, ca. 1891-1932. $400-$600.

Chocolate set, consisting of chocolate pot, 10.5" tall, with four matching cups and saucers. Underglaze factory mark in green, T&V Limoges France, Tressemann & Vogt Mark 7, ca. 1892-1907. $1,000-$1,500.

Chocolate pot, 10" tall, with hand painted chrysanthemums, artist signed "Marsay." Underglaze factory mark in green, Limoges France Mark 6, ca. after 1891. Overglaze decorating mark in blue, Imperial Limoges France Mark, ca. 1800s to early 1900s. $400-$600.

Chocolate pot, 10" tall. Underglaze factory mark in green, J.P.L. France, Jean Pouyat Mark 5, ca. 1890-1932. $400-$600.

Chocolate pot, 9" tall, with hand painted irises and gold base. Underglaze factory mark in green, Haviland & Co. Mark H, ca. 1876-1930. $400-$600.

Chocolate pot, 10" tall. Great example of the *mixtion* process, meaning this pot is partially hand painted. Haviland France, Mark I, ca. 1894-1931. $400-$600.

Salt cellars. Underglaze factory mark in green, AK France, Klingenberg Mark 7, ca. 1890s-1910. $45-$65 each.

Salt and pepper shaker. Unmarked, ca. 1900s-1930. Pair $35-$45.

Salt and pepper shaker.
Unmarked, ca. 1900s-1930.
Pair $35-$45.

Basket, 12.5" long, with artist's initials on the back "MF" and full artist signature "M.G. Fehr" on the front. Underglaze factory mark in green, star with Limoges France, Coiffe Mark 3, ca. after 1891-1914. $295-$395.

Powder sugar shakers, hand painted with floral designs. Underglaze factory mark in green, AK France, Klingenberg Mark 7, ca. 1890s-1910. $65-$195 each.

Basket, 10" long, artist signed "Haste." Underglaze factory mark in green, Limoges France Mark 2, ca. after 1891. $200-$250.

Basket, 8" long, artist signed "J.J. Driscoll" and dated 1910. Underglaze factory mark in green, T&V Limoges France Déposé, Tressemann & Vogt Mark 8, ca. 1907-1919. $95-$125.

Relish tray, 10" long, with gold handles. Underglaze factory mark in green, Limoges France Mark 2, ca. after 1891. $95-$125.

Basket, 8" long, with heavy raised gold. Underglaze factory mark in green, Limoges France Mark 2, ca. after 1891. Overglaze decorating mark in red, Klingenberg and Dwenger Mark 9, ca. 1900-1910. $195-$225.

Rare domed cheese dish, 7" tall with cover. Underglaze factory mark in green, J.P.L. France, Jean Pouyat Mark 5, ca. 1891-1932. $395-$595.

Bowl, 10" diameter. Underglaze factory mark in green, T&V France, Tressemann & Vogt Mark 5a, ca. 1892-1907. $295-$395.

Large nineteenth century French china cabinet with three sections, original glass, and hand painted scenes all around houses a collection of hand painted Limoges. The top is a wonderful spot for massive punch bowls on bases and a tankard with dragon handle. The smaller vitrine in the corner is also perfect for displaying punch bowls.

Cheese dish, 7.5" square. Underglaze factory mark in green, J.P.L. France, Jean Pouyat Mark 5, ca. 1891-1932. $395-$595.

A Venetian glass mirror reflects pieces of beautiful porcelain.

Punch bowl with separate base, 10" x 15", with hand painted roses that extend onto the base. Underglaze factory mark in green, T&V France, Tressemann & Vogt Mark 5a, ca. 1892-1907. $2,500-$3,500.

Punch bowl with separate base, 9.5" x 14", with hand painted roses inside and out. Underglaze factory mark in green, J.P.L. France, Jean Pouyat Mark 5, ca. 1891-1932. $2,000-$3,000.

Punch bowl, 7" tall by 15.5", with matching cups and tray, artist signed "B. Aubin." Underglaze factory mark in green, T&V Limoges France, Tressemann & Vogt Mark 7, ca. 1892-1907. Overglaze decorating mark in gray, L.R.L., Lazeyras, Rosenfeld, and Lehman Mark 3, ca. 1920s. Set $3,500-$5,500.

Matching cup, 3" tall, signed "B. Aubin."

Matching punch bowl tray, 18" diameter, signed "B. Aubin."

Punch bowl, 6" x 14", artist signed "Pierre." Underglaze factory mark in green, three stars and Limoges France, Plainemaison Mark, ca. 1800s-1910. Overglaze mark, Blakeman & Henderson, ca. 1890s. $3,000-$3,500.

Punch bowl on separate base, 9" x 13", with matching cups, hand painted with unique mix of grapes and roses. Underglaze factory mark in green, T&V Limoges France Déposé, Tressemann & Vogt Mark 8, ca. 1907-1919. Set $2,500-$3,000.

Inside of punch bowl above.

Punch bowl on separate base, 9" x 13", with matching cups. Underglaze factory mark in unusual red color, T&V France, Tressemann & Vogt France Mark 5a, ca. 1892-1907. Set $2,500-$3,500.

Massive punch bowl, 8" x 15.5", with hand painted roses. Underglaze factory mark in green, W.G.&Co., France, William Guérin Mark 2, ca. 1891-1900. $2,000-$3,000.

Punch bowl, 4.5" x 9.5", artist signed "N.E. Millard." Underglaze factory mark in green, T&V Limoges France Déposé, Tressemann & Vogt Mark 8, ca. 1907-1919. $900-$1,500.

Punch or fruit bowl, 4.5" x 9.5". Underglaze factory mark in green, T&V Limoges France Déposé, Tressemann & Vogt Mark 8, ca. 1907-1919. Overglaze decorating mark in red, Tressemann & Vogt Mark 16, ca. 1907-1919. $900-$1,500.

Punch bowl, 4.5" x 9.5". Underglaze factory mark in green, T&V Limoges France Déposé, Tressemann & Vogt Mark 8, ca. 1907-1919. Overglaze mark in red with the Picard mark and a paper import sticker. $2,000-$2,200.

Matching undertray for punch bowl on page 134 (bottom right), 14" diameter. Underglaze factory mark in green, Tressemann & Vogt Mark 8, ca. 1907-1919. Overglaze decorating mark in red Tressemann & Vogt Mark 16, ca. 1907-1919. $600-$900.

Fruit bowl on pedestal base, 5.5" x 10". Underglaze factory mark, J.P.L. France, Jean Pouyat Mark 5, ca. 1891-1932. $450-$650.

Fruit bowl, 3.5" x 10". Underglaze factory mark in green, star with Limoges France, Coiffe Mark 2, ca. 1891-1914. $450-$650.

Fruit bowl, 5" x 10". Underglaze factory mark in green, J.P.L. France, Jean Pouyat Mark 5, ca. 1891-1932. $650-$750.

Dining room in a modern home is made romantic and elegant by a low hanging chandelier reflected in this large period mirror. Pieces of porcelain complement the fabric that was used to upholster the chairs.

On the sideboard is a tankard with matching mugs painted with berries similar to that on the punch bowl set below. All pieces in the set are marked with the underglaze factory mark J.P.L. France, Jean Pouyat Mark 5, ca. 1891-1932. Set $1,500-$2,000.

Punch bowl on separate base with matching cups has berries hand painted so well they look real enough to eat. Set $2,000-$2,500.

Tankard, 15" tall. Underglaze factory mark in green, W.G.&Co., Limoges France, William Guérin Mark 3, ca. 1900-1932. $700-$900.

Tankard, 15" tall, with serpent handle. Underglaze factory mark in green, J.P.L. France, Jean Pouyat Mark 5, ca. 1891-1932. $900-$1,200.

Tankard, 15.5" tall, with ornate twisted flower handle. Underglaze factory mark in green, T&V Limoges France, Tressemann & Vogt Mark 7, ca. 1892-1907. $700-$900.

Tankard, 15" tall, with serpent handle, artist signed "Segur" and "Hand painted." Underglaze factory mark in green, J.P.L. France, Jean Pouyat Mark 5, ca. 1891-1932. $1,600-$1,800.

Tankard, 15" tall, with serpent handle. Underglaze factory mark in green, J.P.L. France, Jean Pouyat Mark 5, ca. 1891-1932. $900-$1,200.

Tankard, 15" tall. Underglaze factory mark in green, T&V Limoges France Déposé, Tressemann & Vogt Mark 8, ca. 1907-1919. Overglaze factory mark, Tressemann & Vogt Mark 16, ca. 1907-1919. $700-$900.

Tankard, 14.5" tall, artist signed "Roby" and "Hand painted." Underglaze factory mark in green, J.P.L. France, Jean Pouyat Mark 5, ca. 1891-1932. $1,000-$1,500.

Tankard, 15" tall, artist signed "E.P. Lisby." Underglaze factory mark in green, T&V Limoges France, Tressemann & Vogt Mark 7, ca. 1892-1907. $1,000-$1,200.

Tankard, 14" tall, with illegible artist's signature. Underglaze factory mark in green, Elite/L France, Bawo & Dotter Mark 5, ca. after 1900. Overglaze factory mark in red, Bawo & Dotter Mark 9, ca. 1900-1914. $700-$900.

Tankard or pitcher, 15" tall. Overglaze decorating mark in green, Blakeman & Henderson, ca. 1890s. $700-$900.

Ewer, 14.5" tall. Underglaze factory mark in green, W.G.&Co., France, William Guérin Mark 2, ca. 1891-1900. $700-$900.

Overview of elegant dining room with gold slipcovers that were custom made for the chairs to match the retro draperies. A large marble column is used in a corner to showcase a special vase.

Punch bowl, 4.5" x 11". Underglaze factory mark in green, J.P.L. France, Jean Pouyat Mark, ca. $1,500-$2,000.

Punch bowl, 7" x 16". Underglaze factory mark in green, W.G.&Co., Limoges, France, William Guérin Mark 3, ca. 1900-1932. $1,000-$1,500.

Another view of the same dining room. A floral hand painted punch bowl sits off center on the table.

Cache pot, 12" tall. Underglaze factory mark in green, W.G.&Co., France, William Guérin Mark 2, ca. before 1891-1900. $1,000-$1,200.00

Vase, 8.5" tall. Underglaze factory mark in green, J.P.L. France, Jean Pouyat Mark 5, ca. 1890-1932. $600-$700.

Cache pot, 9" tall. Underglaze factory mark in green, W.G.&Co., Limoges France, William Guérin Mark 3, ca. 1900-1932. $800-$1,000.

Vase, 12" tall. Underglaze factory mark in green, J.P.L. France, with patent date over the top, Jean Pouyat Mark 5, ca. 1890-1932. $800-$1,200.

Vase, 16" tall. Unmarked blank attributed to Limoges. Artist's initials "L.F." $1,500-$2,000.

The shelves house punch bowls, vases of all shapes and sizes, chalices, and teapots.

More shelves, with chocolate pots, tankards, planters, jardinières, cracker jars, and rose bowls.

Elegant table setting of Limoges dinnerware with hand painted violets looks beautiful on this Damask tablecloth.

Custom glass shelves made for wall china cabinets in this dining room make an elegant backdrop for the dining table.

Opposite page, bottom right: Bouillon cup, 2.25" tall, with saucer 6" diameter. Underglaze factory mark in green, Haviland France Mark I, ca. 1894-1931.$75-$195.

Left: Dinner plate, 11.5" diameter. Underglaze factory mark in green, Haviland France Mark I, ca. 1894-1931. $125-$225 each.

Sauce dish, 5.5" diameter. Underglaze factory mark in green, J.P.L. France, Jean Pouyat Mark 5, ca. 1891-1932. $65-$80.

Basket, 12" long. Underglaze factory mark in green, J.P.L. France, Jean Pouyat Mark 5, ca. 1891-1932. $295-$395.

Unusual ewer 11" tall. Overglaze factory mark in red, Bawo & Dotter Mark 8, ca. 1896-1900. $800-$1,200.

Petit vase, 4" tall. Underglaze mark in green, W.G.&Co., Limoges France, William Guérin Mark 3, ca. 1900-1932. $75-$125.

Vase, 12" tall. Underglaze factory mark in green, W.G.&Co., Limoges France, William Guérin Mark 3, ca. 1900-1932. $400-$600.

Vase, 8.5" tall, with ornate double handles. Underglaze factory mark in green, J.P.L. France, Jean Pouyat Mark 5, ca. 1891-1932. $400-$700.

Chalice, 10.5" tall. Underglaze factory mark in green, J.P.L. France, Jean Pouyat Mark 5, ca. 1891-1932. $650-$750.

Squat vase, 8" x 10.5", with beautiful violets. Underglaze factory mark in green, T&V Limoges France, Tressemann & Vogt Mark 7, ca. 1892-1907. $800-$1,500.

Pitcher, 4.75" tall. Underglaze factory mark in green, J.P.L. France, Jean Pouyat Mark 5, ca. 1891-1932. $250-$300.

Pitcher, 3.5" tall, and matching bowl, 6" diameter. Underglaze factory mark in green, H&Co., L France, Haviland Mark F, ca. 1888-1896. $250-$350.

Ferner, 8" tall. Underglaze factory mark in green, Elite L France, Bawo & Dotter Mark 5, ca. after 1900. $600-$800.

Using great decorating style, this small side table in the dining room is perfect for a collection that includes a Limoges lamp with a new shade. Lamp $450-$650.

Tankard, 15" tall with serpent handle, has been made into a lamp. $450-$650.

Lobster set includes platter, 14.5"; five plates, 10" diameter; and gravy boat, 8". Underglaze factory mark in green, Coiffe Mark 3, Flambeau studio. All pieces are marked and artist signed "Dubois." Set $2,500-$3,500.

Gravy boat from the lobster set

This large dining room china cabinet is ideal for unique serving pieces and platters. The lobster set with platter, plates, and sauce dish found the perfect home in this collection.

Platter from the lobster set.

Wedding Band Porcelain

From the beginner to the advanced collector, investing in Wedding Band porcelain dinnerware pieces or completing a set can be very rewarding. Readily available and a bargain in today's Limoges market, this white ware hand painted with a solid gold band is fine Limoges porcelain that was plentiful in the nineteenth century. Imported to the United States as blanks and decorated once here, Wedding Band porcelain was used as everyday dinnerware by the upper middle classes. Many families have inherited complete dinnerware sets, partial sets, and individual pieces of early Haviland and Company and Theodore Haviland. These sets may have had pieces added over generations by various family members.

Haviland did not mark all of their dinnerware until 1871, so it is difficult for a collector to know if a piece is actually from a set manufactured in the Haviland factory or is an inferior piece that was added to a set. Many collectors confuse the later gold banded porcelain of 1894-1931 and incorrectly call it Wedding Band porcelain. Causing more confusion are the many names identifying this porcelain: white ware, wedding ring, wedding band, gold and white, or old Paris Porcelain. But whatever the name, this gold and white Limoges is as desirable today as it was during the Abraham Lincoln and Andrew Jackson administrations.

With understated elegance, the older Wedding Band pieces have patina gold that looks as rich and handsome as if it were wrapped in a piece of 22-karat gold rope. This wonderful Limoges dinnerware symbolizes an era gone by of ostentation and elegance when dinners were events to be shared with family and close friends. Pieces can be found in flea markets and antique shops and are comparatively affordable. White and gold place setting pieces mix easily with most other dinnerware sets and are an lovely addition to a wall.

Old Wedding Band large coffee pot, teapot with matching sugar bowl and creamer, marked Haviland & Company, Marks F & g, ca. 1876-1889. Tea set $275-$325.

Old Wedding Ring butter pat, marked Haviland & Company, Marks F & g, ca. 1876-1889. $10-$25.

Old Wedding Band dinner plate, marked Haviland & Company, Mark F & g, ca. 1876-1889. $25-$35.00

Wedding Band coffee pot, 11" tall. H&Co, Mark B incised on the bottom, ca. 1865. $175-$250.

Old Wedding Band dinner plate, marked Haviland & Company, Mark F & g, ca. 1876-1889. $25-$35.

Opposite page: A nineteenth century cabinet has been in this family for four generations and dramatically showcases the family's beloved Wedding Band Porcelain. The original Old Wedding Band dinnerware is from the 1800s. Generation after generation has added to the set with newer pieces from 1925. Four generations later, the current family members have also added antique pieces to the original set. Pieces have also been hung on the wall, making an elegant wall display.

Old Wedding Band cup and saucer, 2" tall x 5.5 " diameter, marked Haviland & Company, Marks F & g, ca. 1876-1889. $20-$35.

Old Wedding Band cup and saucer, 2" tall x 5" diameter, Wedding Ring design in the bottom of the cup. Marked Haviland & Company, Marks F & g, ca. 1876-1889. $45-$75.

Old Wedding Band demitasse cup and saucer, 2.25" tall x 5" diameter, marked Haviland & Company, Marks F & g, ca. 1876-1889. $35-$45.

The Kitchen

The kitchen is where guests inevitably congregate, so be sure to integrate special Limoges pieces into a conventional kitchen. A china cabinet with a Limoges collection brings individuality to a room that is often furnished in an uninspired way. Draw on techniques that maximize display: use plate rails deep enough to house Limoges punch bowls with their trays standing at the back; hang Limoges platters, chargers, and plates of various sizes on a wall; and place vases filled with fresh roses cut from your garden on the countertops.

Expansive kitchen tables require a massive piece of Limoges or a grouping of Limoges that provides ample scale. In a more intimate kitchen, bring the outdoors in with cheerful floral Limoges pieces that match a sunny outdoor color scheme. Emphasis on a working fireplace in the kitchen contributes to an atmosphere that is warm and inviting. Balance a round Limoges tray and decorative Limoges plates on the mantel with the multiple curves of a wine collection placed in the hearth. Match the colors in the hand painted tile surround with a piece of porcelain. Limoges in any kitchen provides style, inspiration, and personality.

Kitchen eating area coordinates matching fabric on the chairs and window treatment with the Tiffany lighting. A grape theme is consistent in the framed painting and the punch bowl.

Designed with a floor to ceiling china cabinet, the spacious kitchen allows for collections to be contained in one area. Keeping with the grape theme, a large Limoges vase and tankard are placed in a corner.

Punch bowl on original separate base, 9.5" x 13" diameter. Underglaze factory mark in green, T&V Limoges, Déposé, Tressemann & Vogt Mark 6, ca. 1892-1907. Artist's signature on the bottom, "Mrs JH Galloway" and dated 1908. $2,000-2,500.

This spacious modern kitchen has custom cherry cabinets with lights to enhance the Limoges collection, which ranges from dinnerware to decorative pieces.

Mammoth vase, 16" tall and 32" in circumference. Underglaze factory mark in green, D&C, Délinières Mark 1, ca. 1870s. $1,500-$2,000.

Jardinière, 8" tall. Underglaze factory mark in green, D&C France, Délinières & Co., Mark 3, ca. 1894-1900. $1,500-$2,000.

This kitchen has a wonderful open sitting area that brings the gardens inside.

A Limoges vase holds freshly cut garden flowers, complementing the hand painted flowers on the front of the vase. Underglaze factory mark in green, W.G.&Co., Limoges France, William Guérin Mark 3, ca. 1900-1932. $600-$800.

Kitchen eating area houses an oak china cabinet with glass doors showing off a beautiful Limoges collection that consists of hand painted and artist signed "Andrew" pieces.

Bonbon dish, 8.75" x 6". Underglaze factory mark in green, J.P.L France, Jean Pouyat, Mark 5, ca. 1890-1932. Artist's signature on the front, "Andrew." $80-$120.

Charger, 14" diameter, with heavy gold scalloped rim. Underglaze factory mark in green, T&V Limoges France, Tressemann & Vogt Mark 7, ca. 1892-1907. Artist's signature on the front, "Andrew." $700-$900.

Charger, 15" diameter. Underglaze factory mark in green, T&V Limoges France, Tressemann & Vogt Mark 7, ca. 1892-1907. Artist's signature on the front, "Andrew." $700-$900.

Covered soup tureen, 13" diameter. Underglaze factory mark in green, H&Co., L/France, Haviland & Co., Mark H, ca. 1888-1896. Artist's signature, "Andrew." $800-$1,000.

Covered soup tureen, 8" x 9". Underglaze mark in green, P and P, Paroutaud Frères, Mark 2, ca. 1903-1917. Artist's signature on the cover, "Andrew." $900-$1,500.

Compote, 9" x 10", artist's signature, "Andrew." Underglaze factory mark in green, H&Co., L/France, Haviland & Co., Mark H, ca. 1888-1896. $650-$750.

Covered soup tureen, 9" x 13", hand painted ocean blue with a dolphin finial on the cover and matching set of eight bowls. Underglaze mark in green, W.G.&Co., France, William Guérin Mark 2, before 1891-1900. Overglaze decorating mark in red, W.G.&Co., France, William Guérin Mark 3, ca. before 1891—a very rare decorating mark. Set $2,000-$2,500.

Matching soup bowls, all marked as stated.

Fabulous cobalt and gold ice cream set in its original Victorian presentation case. Underglaze factory mark in green, Haviland Mark H, ca. 1888-1896. Overglaze decorating mark in red, Mark g. Set in case, $2,800-$3,000.

Matching ice cream bowl, 4" x 4".

The ice cream platter, 9" x 12".

Ice cream bowl or plate, 6" x 6". Underglaze factory mark in green, AL with anchor and Limoges, France, Lanternier Mark 4, ca. 1891-1914. Overglaze decorating mark in blue with Limoges France in a double circle, Lanternier Mark 6, ca. 1891-1914. Import mark, WL HELM & GRAFF. Set $500-$650.

This kitchen had custom cherry cabinets built with a "plate rail" specifically high and wide enough to house a large Limoges punch bowl collection. The bowls are safely displayed out of reach of small children and pets.

A rare German oak chocolate cabinet with etched glass houses punch bowl cups and other pieces of a fabulous porcelain collection.

Punch bowl on base, 9.5" x 14", with six cups. Set is marked with the underglaze factory mark in green, T&V Limoges France, Tressemann & Vogt Mark 7, ca. 1892-1907. Set 3,000-$3,500.

Punch bowl on base, 9.5" x 14", with matching tray, 15.5" diameter. All three pieces have matching underglaze marks in green, T&V Limoges France, Tressemann & Vogt Mark 7, ca. 1892-1907. Overglaze artist's signature and marks "SE Blanchard, Lynn, 1900." Set $3,000-$3,500.

Punch bowl, 7" x 14", on a base with six cups. Underglaze factory mark in green, W.G.&Co., Limoges France, Guérin Mark 3; base underglaze factory mark in green, T&V Limoges France, Tressemann & Vogt Mark 7, ca. 1892-1907. Set $1,500-$2,000.

Punch cup, 5.25" tall. Underglaze factory mark in green, T&V Limoges France, Tressemann & Vogt, Mark 7, ca. 1892-1907. $20-$25 each.

Punch bowl on base, both with heavy gold, 9.5" x 14", matching set of twelve cups. Underglaze factory mark in green, W.G.&Co., Limoges France, William Guérin Mark 3, ca. 1900-1932. Set $2,500-$3,500.

Massive punch bowl on base, 7" x 16", with twelve matching cups; oval tray, 16" diameter. All pieces marked underglaze T&V Limoges France, Tressemann & Vogt, Mark 7, ca. 1892-1907. Set $3,500-$4,000.

Punch cup, 5.1" tall. Underglaze factory mark in green, T&V Limoges France, Tressemann & Vogt Mark 7, ca. 1892-1907. $50-$75 each.

Punch bowl on base, 9.5" x 13.5". Underglaze factory mark in green, T&V Limoges France, Tressemann & Vogt Mark 7, ca. 1892-1907. $2,500-$3,000.

Punch bowl on base, 9.5" x 14", with tray, 16" diameter, and six matching cups. All pieces marked underglaze with T&V Limoges France, Tressemann & Vogt, Mark 7, ca. 1892-1907. Set $2,500-$3,500.

Punch bowl with base, 9.5" x 14", scalloped rim. Underglaze factory mark in green, T&V Limoges France, Tressemann & Vogt Mark 7, ca. 1892-1907. $2,500-$3,000.

Punch cup, 4.9" tall. Underglaze factory mark in green, T&V Limoges France, Tressemann & Vogt Mark 7, ca. 1892-1907. $50-$75 each.

Punch bowl on base, 9.5" x 13.5". Underglaze factory mark in green, T&V Limoges France, Tressemann & Vogt Mark 7, ca. 1892-1907. $2,500-$3,000.

Punch cup, 4.5" tall, with handle. Underglaze factory mark in green, T&V Limoges France, Tressemann & Vogt Mark 7, ca. 1892-1907. $100-$125 each.

Punch bowl, 6" x 12", and tray, 12" diameter. Matching set marked with the underglaze factory mark in green, T&V Limoges France, Tressemann & Vogt Mark 7, ca. 1892-1907. Set $2,000-$2,500.

Punch bowl, 7" x 16", unusually large blank. Underglaze factory mark in green, T&V Limoges France, Tressemann & Vogt, Mark 7, ca. 1892-1907. $2,000-$2,500.

Above and below: Punch bowl, 7" x 14", on four gold legs with matching tray, 16" diameter. Matching set with underglaze factory mark in green, T&V Limoges France, Tressemann & Vogt, Mark 7, ca. 1892-1907. Set $3,000-$4,000.

Tray, 16" diameter. Underglaze mark in green, T&V Limoges France, Tressemann & Vogt, Mark 7, ca. 1892-1907. $1,000-$1,500.

Punch bowl, 14.5" diameter. Underglaze factory mark in green, T&V Limoges France, Tressemann & Vogt Mark 7, ca. 1892-1907. $1,000-$1,500.

Punch bowl, 7" x 16", unusually large blank. Underglaze factory mark in green, T&V Limoges France, Tressemann & Vogt, Mark 7, ca 1892-1907. $2,000-$2,500.

Inside of punch bowl above, beautifully hand painted with spider web.

Punch bowl, 13.5" diameter. Underglaze factory mark in green, Limoges France Mark 6, ca. after 1891. $1,000-$1,500.

Punch bowl, 14.5" diameter. Underglaze factory mark in green, T&V Limoges France Déposé, Tressemann & Vogt Mark 8, ca. 1907-1919. $1,000-$1,500.

Punch bowl, 13" diameter. Underglaze factory mark in green, T&V Limoges France, Tressemann & Vogt Mark 7, ca. 1892-1907. $800-$1,500.

Punch bowl, 7" x 14", on four gold legs. Underglaze factory mark in green, T&V Limoges France, Tressemann & Vogt Mark 7, ca. 1892-1907. $2,000-$3,000.

This kitchen fireplace has a green marble and porcelain fireplace surround with hand painted flowers on each tile. The mantel houses an unusual Limoges chalice and plates that complement the tile motif. Limoges vases and tankards are nearby.

Set of six matching dessert plates, 8.5" diameter. Factory decorated, hand painted, and artist's signature "Magne." Underglaze factory mark in green, Limoges France, Mark 1, ca. 1891 and after. Overglaze decorating mark in red, Ovington Bro's New York. Set $600-$800.

Chalice, 10" tall, hand painted with roses and portrait of Victorian woman. Artist's signature "S.N.Fanar." Underglaze factory mark in green, T&V Limoges France, Tressemann & Vogt Mark 7, ca. 1892-1907. $600-$800.

Mammoth vase, 22.5" tall, artist signed "K.Blissel" and dated 1912. Underglaze factory mark in green, T&V Limoges France, Tressemann & Vogt Mark 7, ca. 1892-1907. $1,700-$2,200.

Chalice, 10" tall, dripping gold gilt and enameled roses. Underglaze mark in green, T&V Limoges France, Tressemann & Vogt Mark 7, ca., 1892-1907. $600-$800.

This eat in kitchen uses fifteen unique Limoges plates as a border overhanging the entrance between rooms.

Casual dining in the kitchen can be romantic when using a hand painted Limoges rose luncheon set.

Bowl, 12" diameter, artist signed "J.Golse." Underglaze factory mark in green, star with Limoges France, Coiffe Mark 3, ca. 1891-1914. Overglaze decorating mark, H&Co., Mark g, ca. 1879-1889. $450-$500.

Plate, 9" diameter; matching cup, 4.5"; and saucer, 6" diameter. Underglaze factory mark in green, H&Co., L/France, Haviland Mark H, ca. 1888-1896. $295 each.

Bonbon dish, 8.5" x 6". Underglaze factory mark in green, W.G.&Co., Limoges France, William Guérin Mark 3, ca. 1900-1932. $70-$90.

Celery or relish tray, 12" long. Underglaze factory mark in green, P.M. Mavaleix mark, ca. 1908-1914. $125-$225.

Dessert in this kitchen might be fresh fruit served in a berry bowl and sweets served on a hand painted cake plate with matching dessert plates, each uniquely hand painted.

Serving tray, 12.5" x 9". Underglaze factory mark in green, J.P.L. France, Jean Pouyat Mark 5, ca. 1890-1932. $395-$495.

Cake plate, 11" diameter, with six dessert plates, 9" diameter each. All pieces in this matching set have illegible artist's initials and are marked with the J.P.L. France, Jean Pouyat Mark 5, ca. 1891-1932, underglaze factory mark in green. Set $600-$800.

Set of six matching dessert plates, 9" diameter, with unusual hand painted floral designs. Underglaze mark in green, T&V, Tressemann & Vogt Mark 4, ca. early 1890s. Set $550-$650.

The Bedroom or Boudoir

The privacy and romance of a bedroom invites art and Limoges collections with special meaning—make the master suite an inviting retreat worth retiring to. Floral drapes complemented by floral Limoges vases provide a garden of colors and comfortable charm. Dark walls wrap a room in warmth and allow savoring of your favorite Limoges pieces. Papered or painted bedroom walls become canvases dedicated to a collage of Limoges.

Hang Limoges plaques signed by French listed artists over a bed. Mix a dresser tray that complements a favorite piece of framed art and hang your framed Limoges painting on porcelain on the wall. A misplaced tourine cover found at a flea market and some dessert plates provide an inexpensive way to personalize your room.

Limoges accessories flatter a bedroom while a lamp provides the balance framework for a collection of Limoges dresser sets, hair receivers, and brushes. Tiny vignettes of brooches, hatpins, and buttons make sweet dreams come easy.

Plaque, 12" diameter, produced in a factory in Limoges and decorated in another. Overglaze decorating mark is the Coronet, Limoges France with a crown, George Borgfeldt Mark 1, ca. 1906-1920. Artist's signature on front "Ramon." $800-$1,000.

Plaque, 14" diameter. Overglaze decorating mark, Coronet, Limoges France with a crown, George Borgfeldt Mark 1, ca. 1906-1920. Signature of factory listed artist "A. Bronssillon" on front. $1,200-$1,400.

Plaque, 14" diameter. Overglaze decorating mark, Coronet, Limoges France with a crown, George Borgfeldt Mark 1, ca. 1906-1920. Signature of factory listed artist "A. Bronssillon" on front. $1,200-$1,500.

Plaque, 13" diameter, with thick heavy gold gilt on edges. Overglaze decorating mark, Coronet, Limoges France with crown, George Borgfeldt Mark 1, ca. 1906-1920. Signature of factory listed artist "A. Bronssillon" on front. $900-$1,200.

Plaque, 14" diameter. Overglaze decorating mark, Coronet, Limoges France with crown, George Borgfeldt Mark 1, ca. 1906-1920. Signature of factory listed artist "A. Bronssillon" on front. $1,200-$1,500.

Opposite page: All romance and roses, this bedroom has walls filled with nineteenth century Limoges plaques signed by listed French artists surrounding a nineteenth century needlepoint tapestry. Limoges lamps provide the perfect lighting.

Plaque, 14" diameter. Overglaze decorating mark, Coronet, Limoges France with crown, George Borgfeldt Mark 1, ca. 1906-1920. Signature of factory listed artist "A. Bronssillon" on front. One of a pair, $1,200-$1,500 each.

Plaque, 14" diameter. Underglaze factory mark in green, torch with Limoges France, Flambeau Marks 1, ca. 1890s-1914. Overglaze decorating mark in red, torch with Limoges France, Flambeau Mark 2, ca. 1890s. $400-$600.

Plaque, 14" diameter. Overglaze decorating mark in red, torch with Limoges France, Flambeau Mark 2, ca. 1890s. $600-$800.

Plaque, 13.5" diameter, artist signed "René." Overglaze decorating mark in red, torch with Limoges France, Flambeau China mark 4, ca. 1890s-1900s. $600-$800.

Plaque, 14" diameter. Underglaze factory mark in green, torch with Limoges France, Flambeau China Mark 1, ca. 1890s-1914. Overglaze decorating mark in red, torch with Limoges France, Flambeau Mark 3, ca. 1890s-1900s. $800-$1,200.

Large lamp, 28" tall. Underglaze factory mark, W.G.&Co., Limoges France, William Guérin Mark 3, ca. 1900-1932. $800-$1,000.

Jardinière, 9" tall, includes the separate base height. Gold gilt hand painted lions' head handles and paw feet, with roses all around. Underglaze factory mark in green, D&C France, Délinières & Co., Mark 3, ca. 1894-1900. $1,500-$2,000.

Lamp, 24" tall, artist signed "René." Underglaze factory mark, W.G.&Co., Limoges France, William Guérin Mark 3, ca. 1900-1932. $800-$1,200.

High ceilings in this bedroom allow for a grouping of Limoges chargers above an oversized, quarter sawn oak Victorian bed with applied carvings. A tea table, Limoges tea set, and biscuit jar on tea tray are inviting on a hand-crocheted bedspread.

This collector houses pieces of her Limoges collection on top of a rare Victorian humidor with marble top and Limoges hand painted insets on the front of the doors. Nineteenth century pieces of furniture of this caliber are valued between $2,500-$5,000, depending on overall condition and whether the piece has its original marble.

Limoges insert on the left door.

The top of this oak dresser displays a Limoges glove and hankie box, miniature pieces of art in the form of hand painted buttons, and a rare Limoges picture and thermometer frame.

Limoges insert on the right door.

Charger, 15" diameter, with irregular scalloped edges and gold border. Underglaze mark in green, AK over D with France, Klingenberg and Dwenger Mark 7, ca. 1890-1910. $800-$1,000.

Charger, 14" diameter. Underglaze factory mark in green, AK over D with France, Klingenberg and Dwenger Mark 7, ca. 1890-1910. $800-1,000.

Lamp, 18" tall. Underglaze factory mark in green, D&Co., France, Délinières & Co., Mark 3, ca. 1894-1900. $1,800-$2,200.

Charger, 15" diameter. Underglaze factory mark in green, AK over D with France, Klingenberg and Dwenger Mark 7, ca. 1890-1910. $800-$1,000.

Hankie or dresser box, 3" tall x 8" square. Underglaze factory mark in green, D&Co., France, Délinières & Co., Mark 3, ca. 1894-1900. $250-$450.

Glove or dresser box, 2" x 15" long, matches the hankie box . Underglaze factory mark in green, D&Co., France, Délinières & Co., Mark 3, ca. 1894-1900. $350-$550.

Cuspidor, 7" x 9", hand painted. Underglaze mark in green, H. & Co., underscored, Haviland & Co., Mark D, ca. 1877. $500-$600.

Jardinière, 10" tall, 32" in circumference at widest point. Underglaze factory mark in green, D&Co., France, Délinières & Co., Mark 3, ca. 1894-1900. Artist's initials "E.W.P." and dated 1898. $2,000-$2,200.

Painting on porcelain, 7" x 6", in original frame, 10" x 11". Underglaze factory mark in green, T&V France, Tressemann & Vogt, Mark 5a, ca. 1892-1907. Artist's initials "E.A.J." with written instructions for framing on the back. $1,200-$1,500.

Nineteenth century kidney shaped tea table made from burl wood. The table has four bronze ormolu mounts with hand painted Limoges inserts on all sides. Table in pristine condition $4,800-$5,200.

Lamp, 12" tall. Underglaze factory mark in green, B&C France, Mark 1, ca. 1900-1914. Overglaze decorating mark, Picard. $1,800-$2,200.

Close-ups of the four hand painted Limoges table inserts depicting romantic courting scenes.

Dresser jar, 2.5" x 7". Heavy gold with raised enameled blue dots and roses in a scrolled cameo insert. Underglaze factory mark in green, T&V Limoges France, Tressemann & Vogt, Mark 7, ca. 1892-1907. $600-$700.

Spacious bedroom has large living area that needs large accent pieces.

Plaque, 18" diameter, portrait of young maiden, artist signed "Dubois." Overglaze decorating mark, torch with Limoges France, Flambeau Mark 2, ca. 1890s. $2,500-$3,000.

One from a pair of Limoges lamps, 14" tall. Underglaze factory mark in green, T&V Limoges France, Tressemann & Vogt Mark 7, ca. 1892-1907. Pair $1,000-$1,500.

Plaque, 18" diameter, portrait of a woman, artist signed "Dubois." Overglaze decorating mark, torch with Limoges France, Flambeau Mark 2, ca. 1890s. $2,500-$3,000.

Oval painting on porcelain, 18". Underglaze factory mark in green, T&V Limoges France, Tressemann & Vogt Mark 7, ca. 1892-1907. $900-$1,200.

Vase, 13", tall, portrait of a woman in heavy raised gold cameo, artist's initials "E.T.S." and dated 1888. Underglaze factory mark in green, J.P.L., Jean Pouyat Mark 3, ca. 1862-1900s. $1,400-$1,500.

Top right: Plaque, 14" diameter. Overglaze decorating mark in gray, Lazeyras, Rosenfeld & Lehman Mark 3, ca. 1920s. $700-$900.

Bottom right: Plaque, 15" diameter, with ornate gilding. Overglaze decorating mark in green, Blakeman & Henderson, ca. 1890s. $600-$800.

Plaque, 16" diameter, vibrant detailed portrait of birds. Overglaze decorating mark in gray, Lazeyras, Rosenfeld & Lehman Mark 3, ca. 1920s. $1,200-$1,500.

A large bedroom has room in a tiny corner to display a beloved collection of Limoges pieces with hand painted poppies.

Large bulbous vase, 14" tall, portrait of lovers. Underglaze factory mark in green, J.P.L. France, Jean Pouyat Mark 5, ca. 1890-1932. $1,500-$1,900.

Dessert plate, 9" diameter, with vivid hand painted poppies. Overglaze decorating mark, Coronet, George Borgfeldt, Mark 1, ca. 1906-1920. $35-$45.

Romance and love emanate from this welcoming Victorian bedroom. Frilly Scottish lace curtains make the perfect backdrop for this beautiful vase and portrait plate.

The wallpaper in this charming bedroom was chosen to complement the vintage bedspread and Limoges collection of pansies and violets.

Vase, 12" tall. Overglaze decorating mark, "Picard." $600-$800.

As shown, a wall can be decorated with a collection of Limoges hand painted dessert and cake plates. Add an odd lid and you have a unique wall for less than $200. Use transfer ware dessert plates and your wall can cost under $50.

Vase, 18" tall, in Art Deco style. Underglaze factory mark in green, J.P.L. France, Jean Pouyat Mark 5, ca. 1891-1932. $1,500-$1,700.

Tray, 10" diameter. Underglaze factory mark in green, W.G.&Co., William Guérin Mark 3, ca. 1900-1932. $295-$395.

Limoges punch bowl, 16" x 9.5". Underglaze factory mark in green, Elite/L/France, Bawo & Dotter Marks 5 and 9, ca. 1900s. $1,900-$2,000.

Covered jar, 10" long. Underglaze factory mark in green, AK France, Klingenberg Mark 7, ca. 1890s-1910. $600-$700.

A bedroom with rustic beamed ceilings has a wall covering designed to enhance the lovely pink and green colors of this collector's Limoges vases.

Vase, 12" tall, with flamboyant gold handles. Underglaze factory mark in green, W.G.&Co., Limoges France, William Guérin, Mark 3, ca. 1900-1932. $500-$700.

Vase, 14" tall, with small neck. Underglaze factory mark in green, T&V Limoges France, Tressemann & Vogt, Mark 7, ca. 1892-1907. $800-$1,200.

Vase, 16" tall, artist signed "Anna Peters Denver." Underglaze factory mark in green, D&Co., Délinières & Co., Mark 1, ca. 1870s. $1,000-$1,300.

Vase, 13" tall, artist signed "P.Putzki." Underglaze factory mark in green, J.P. L. France, Jean Pouyat Mark 5, ca. 1891-1932. $800-$1,200.

Vase, 16" tall, with heavy gold rim. Underglaze factory mark in green, W.G.&Co., Limoges France, William Guérin Mark 3, ca. 1900-1932. $1,200-$1,500.

Vase, 13" tall, artist signed "Ruby Griffith." Underglaze mark in green, GDA France, Gérard, Dufraisseix , and Abbot Mark 1, ca. 1900-1941. $800-$1,200.

Displayed in this bedroom are small collections composed of loved hand painted hatpins, stick pins, and brooches.

Victorian sitting table with marble top has a lovely display of hand painted hatpins in a Limoges hatpin holder. Antique Limoges hatpins, ca. 1890s-1930s. $275-$475 each.

Limoges dresser set with brush, mirror, and comb. Underglaze mark, W.G.&Co., Limoges France, Guérin Mark 3, ca. 1900-1932. Matching set $600-$700.

Limoges vase, 13.5" tall. Underglaze factory mark in green, W.G.&Co., Limoges France, Guérin Mark 3, ca. 1900-1932. $900-$1,200.

Mirror, 8" long, artist signed "Petit." Original backing on mirrors prevents seeing manufacturing marks, but this mirror is ca. 1890s-1930s. $150-$250.

Mirror, 8" long, artist signed "Petit," ca. 1890s-1930s. $150-$250.

Mirror, 8" long, artist signed "Girsard," ca. 1890s-1930s. $150-$250.

Mirror, 8" long, artist signed "Merville," ca. 1890s-1930s. $150-$250.

Limoges dresser sets are delightful to collect. The trays come in all different shapes and sizes and some sets include covered powder jars, hair receivers, candlestick holders, button boxes, and hatpin holders. This set includes a tray, covered powder jar, and hair receiver. Sets range from $395 to $1,295.

Hair receiver, 2.25" x 3.75" diameter. Underglaze factory mark in green, W.G.&Co., France, Guérin Mark 1, ca. 1891-1900. $100-$200.

Covered powder jar, 4.25" x 2.25", ornate gold top. Underglaze factory mark in green, W.G.&Co., France Guérin Mark 1, ca. 1891-1900. $150-$250.

Tray, 9" x 12", with raised gold paste. Underglaze factory mark in green, W.G.&Co., France, Guérin, Mark 1, ca. 1891-1900. $295-$395.

Complete Limoges dresser set. All pieces have matching factory underglaze mark in green, T&V Limoges France, Tressemann & Vogt, Mark 7, ca. 1892-1907. Set $395-$1,295.

Hair receiver, 2.25" x 3.75". Underglaze factory mark in green, T&V Limoges France, Tressemann & Vogt, Mark 7, ca. 1892-1907. $100-$200.

Limoges tray with unusual shape, 12" x 14". Underglaze factory mark in green, T&V Limoges France, Tressemann & Vogt Mark 7, ca. 1892-1907. $195-$295.

Covered powder jar, 2.25" x 3.75". Underglaze factory mark in green, T&V Limoges France, Tressemann & Vogt, Mark 7, ca. 1892-1907. $100-$150.

Limoges dresser set, all pieces marked with the underglaze factory mark in green, W.G.&Co., France, William Guérin Mark 1, ca. 1891-1900. Set $400-$900.

Hair receiver, 2" x 3". Underglaze factory mark in green, W.G.&Co., France, William Guérin, Mark 1, ca. 1891-1900. $95-$125.

Covered powder jar, 2" x 3". Underglaze factory mark in green, W.G.&Co., France, William Guérin, Mark 1, ca. 1891-1900. $50-$100.

Tray with handles, 9" x 12". Underglaze factory mark in green, W.G.&Co., France, William Guérin Mark 1, ca. 1891-1900. $195-$295.

Dresser tray, 10" long, on four gold legs. Underglaze factory mark in green, PL Limoges France, La Porcelaine Limousine Mark 1, ca. 1905-1930. $195-$295.

Hair receiver, 5.5" diameter. Underglaze factory mark in green, PL Limoges France, La Porcelaine Limousine Mark 1, ca. 1905-1930. $100-$175.

Candlesticks, 8.5" tall. Underglaze factory mark in green, PL Limoges France, La Porcelaine Limousine Mark 1, ca. 1905-1930. $195-$295.

Bottom right: Covered powder jar, 6.5" diameter. Underglaze factory mark in green, PL Limoges France, La Porcelaine Limousine Mark 1, ca. 1905-1930. $100-$200.

Dresser tray, 14" diameter. Underglaze factory mark in green, T&V Limoges, France, Tressemann & Vogt, Mark 7, ca. 1892-1907. $395-$695.

Square covered box , 3" tall x 5.5" square. Underglaze factory mark in green, PL Limoges France, La Porcelaine Limousine Mark 1, ca. 1905-1930. $150-$250.

Candlestick, 12" tall. Underglaze factory mark in green, PL Limoges France, La Porcelaine Limousine Mark 1, ca. 1905-1930. $150-$200.

Dresser box , 2.75" x 3.75". Underglaze factory mark in green, PL Limoges France, La Porcelaine Limousine Mark 1, ca. 1905-1930. $125-$175.

The Bathroom or Powder Room

The bathroom can be intimate and charming without being serious. Limoges in the bathroom is a great choice because it is unexpected. Furniture that complements Limoges accessories make the bath as sophisticated as any other room in the home.

Hand painted sinks make a decorative accessory to complement a piece of Limoges. Introduce Limoges lamps and make a bathroom less sterile and more personable. Countertops become less conventional when a Limoges vase becomes the focal point. With doors left open, a linen cabinet becomes a natural haven for a Limoges collection. An open shelf or a small antique table can hold Limoges trays, bottles, and jars. A needlepoint chair and rug complement the floral theme of the Limoges and introduce personality in a room that is usually overlooked.

Vase, 11.5" tall, with large hand painted roses and unusual handles. Underglaze factory mark in green, Haviland France, Haviland & Co. Mark Q, ca. 1894-1931. $900-$1,200.

Brilliant red bathroom is decorated with a large 14" jardinière. Underglaze factory mark in green, W.G.&Co., France, William Guérin Mark 2, ca. 1891-1900. $1,500-$2,000.

A hand painted sink and dark green ceramic tiles showcase lovely Limoges vases reflected in the large modern bathroom mirror. This room is a great example of how you can mix modern and whimsy art with your Limoges.

Vase, 9.5" tall, with gold gilt handles. Underglaze factory mark in green, W.G.&Co., France, Guérin Mark 2, ca. 1891-1900. $400-$600.

Wisteria, lilacs, and violets are all reflective of the Victorians' love for purple and fascination with royalty. This regal powder room is perfect for hand painted, decorative Limoges pieces with purple flowers.

Dresser set, including matching tray, covered powder jar, and hair receiver. Hand painted violets encased in raised gold paste enhance the beauty of this set. Underglaze factory mark in green, J.P.L. France, Jean Pouyat Mark 5, ca. 1890-1932. Set $600-$800.

Large Limoges vases are perfect for bringing the garden into your living quarters and are captivating in intimate rooms.

Painting on porcelain, lovely violets in three porcelain 6" x 6" squares, in original frame. Underglaze factory mark in green, T&V Limoges, Tressemann & Vogt Mark 4b, ca. 1892-1907. $250-$400.

Large vase, 15" tall, has six panels hand painted with various shades of purple lilacs and dripping gold. Underglaze factory mark in green, D&C France, Délinières & Co., Mark 3, ca. 1894-1900. $2,000-$2,500.

Ferner, 3.5" x 8", with liner. Underglaze factory mark in green, AK France, Klingenberg Mark 8, ca. 1890-1910. $400-$500.

In this true collector's powder room, the wash basin has been hand painted to match a jardinière on the countertop. Vases, cachepots, powder jars, trays, chargers, and paintings on porcelain are all displayed in this fun room. The wallpaper and blinds have been chosen to enhance the collection and pieces are reflected in a Victorian beveled glass, hand painted mirror.

Cachepots range from 6" to 12" tall. Their potential uses range from desk accessories to waste holders to planters and vases.

Cachepots used for hand towels and tissue. Powder jars and trays hold lovely hand painted brooches and pendants and hair receivers house cotton balls.

Cachepot, 11" tall, with gold handles and feet. Underglaze factory mark in green, W.G.&Co., Limoges France, William Guérin Mark 3, ca. 1900-1932. $1,100-$1,200.

Cachepot, 11" tall, with gold handles and feet. Underglaze factory mark in green, W.G.&Co., Limoges France, William Guérin Mark 3, ca. 1900-1932. $1,100-$1,200.

Cachepot, 9" tall, with gold handles and feet. Underglaze factory mark in green, W.G.&Co., Limoges France, William Guérin Mark 3, ca. 1900-1932. $800-$1,000.

Jardinière, 11" tall, with gold gilt around rim, beautiful roses, and matching tray. Underglaze factory mark in green, W.G.&Co., Limoges France, William Guérin Mark 3, ca. 1900-1932. $1,000-$1,600 with tray.

Cachepot, 12" tall, with gold handles and feet. Underglaze factory mark in green, W.G.&Co., Limoges France, William Guérin Mark 3, ca. 1900-1932. $1,200-$1,500.

Jardinière, 11" tall, with gold rim. Underglaze factory mark in green, D&Co., France, Délinières & Co., Mark 3, ca. 1894-1900. $800-$1,200.

Jardinière, 9" tall. Underglaze factory mark in green, W.G.&Co., Limoges France, William Guérin Mark 3, ca. 1900-1932. $800-$1,200.

Large powder jar, 5.5" x 9.5". Underglaze factory mark in green, T&V Limoges France, Tressemann & Vogt Mark 7, ca. 1892-1907. $350-$550.

Jardinière, 7.5" tall. Underglaze factory mark in green, T&V Limoges France, Tressemann & Vogt Mark 7, ca. 1892-1907. $600-$800.

Powder jar, 5.5" x 6.5", heavily gilded. Underglaze factory mark in green, T&V Limoges France, Tressemann & Vogt Mark 7, ca. 1892-1907. $350-$550.

Hair receiver, 3.5" x 4", artist's initials "F.K.T." Underglaze factory mark in green, T&V Limoges France, Tressemann & Vogt Mark 7, ca. 1892-1907. $100-$350.

Powder bowl or jar, 5.5" x 6.5". Underglaze factory mark in green, B&Co., France, Bernardaud & Co., Mark 1, ca. 1900-1914. $375-$450.

Powder jar or trinket box, 5.5" x 6.5". Underglaze factory mark in green, Elite/L/France, Bawo & Dotter Mark 5, ca. after 1900. $350-$400.

Painting on porcelain, 4.5" x 6.5", in original frame. Underglaze factory mark in green, D&Co., France, Délinières & Co. Mark 3, ca. 1894-1900. $600-$1,000.

Painting on porcelain, 7.5" oval, in original frame. Underglaze factory mark in green, J.P.L. France, Jean Pouyat Mark 5, ca. 1890-1932. $1,000-$1,200.

Painting on porcelain, 9" x 11", in original frame. Underglaze factory mark in green, J.P.L. France, Jean Pouyat Mark 5, ca. 1890-1932. $1,200-$1,500.

Painting on porcelain, 11" x 14", in the original frame that has been painted gold. Underglaze factory mark in green, T&V Limoges France, Tressemann & Vogt Mark 7, ca. 1892-1907. $2,000-$2,500.

This Gothic Revival home has the first bathroom that was documented in historic Rowley, Massachusetts to have indoor plumbing. Embellished with a few magnificent pieces of Limoges art, it has been kept as true to the period as possible.

Tray, 16" diameter. Underglaze factory mark in green, GDM France, Gérard, Dufraisseix , and Morel Mark 2, ca. 1891-1900. Artist signed "Eva Lemon Clark for Columbian Expo" and dated 1893. $1,000-1,500.

Large tray, 16" diameter. Underglaze factory mark in green, T&V Limoges France, Tressemann & Vogt, Mark 7, ca. 1892-1907. Artist's initials "E.D.S." and dated 1913. $900-$1,200.

Tray, 14" diameter. Underglaze factory mark in green, GDM France, Gérard, Dufraisseix , and Morel Mark 2, ca. 1891-1900. $500-$700.

Large tray, 16" diameter. Underglaze factory mark in green, T&V Limoges France, Tressemann & Vogt, Mark 7, ca. 1892-1907. $900-$1,200.

Large tray, 16" diameter. Underglaze factory mark in green, T&V Limoges France, Tressemann & Vogt, Mark 7, ca. 1892-1907. Artist signed "To Carl From Mary Xmas 1907." $900-$1,200.

Newly remodeled powder room is enhanced by pieces of Limoges art nestled amongst Victorian prints on the wall. Individual plates like these range from $25-$175.

Vase, 14" tall. Underglaze factory mark in green, J.P.L. Limoges France, Jean Pouyat Mark 5, ca. 1890-1932. $1,200-$1,500.

On the countertop, hand painted and artist signed Limoges trays are displayed proudly on Victorian brass stands. These tiny treasures run from $20-$395.

Pin tray, 4" x 6". Impressed initials of T&H, Theodore Haviland Mark. Overglaze decorating mark in red script, slanted Theodore Haviland Limoges France, Mark p, ca. 1903-1925. Artist's signature on front "Armand." $90-$125.

Tray, 11" x 6", with split center handle. Underglaze factory mark in green, W.G.& Co., Limoges France, William Guérin Mark 3, ca. 1900-1932. $295-$395.

Pin tray, 5" x 6.5". Underglaze factory mark in green, Limoges France Mark 2, ca. after 1891. Overglaze mark in red, "hand painted" and artist's signature "Sena" on front. $90-$125.00

Dresser tray, 12" x 9", with irregular scalloped shape. Underglaze factory mark in green, W.G.&Co., France, William Guérin Mark 2, ca. 1891-1900. $250-$350.

Tray, 12.5 x 9", ornate with pierced handles. Underglaze factory mark in green, J.P.L. France, Jean Pouyat Mark 5, ca. 1890-1932. $300-$395.

Tray, 11" x 6", with split center handle. Underglaze factory mark in green, W.G.&Co., Limoges France, William Guérin Mark 3, ca. 1900-1932. $295-$395.

Tiny dresser or pin tray, 3.5" x 4.5". This unmarked tray is part of a dresser set with the Guérin Mark 3. $20-$60.

Dresser tray, 12.5" x 8". Underglaze factory mark in green, T&V Limoges France, Tressemann & Vogt Mark 7, ca. 1892-1907. $200-$295.

Tray, 10" x 8", with unusual scalloped edges. Underglaze factory mark in green, J.P.L. France, Jean Pouyat Mark 5a, ca. 1890-1932. $300-$395.

Ornate dresser tray, 11.5" x 8.5". Underglaze factory mark in green, T&V Limoges France, Tressemann & Vogt, Mark 7, ca. 1892-1907. $295-$395.

Part III

Wearing Your Limoges

Button, button who has the button? Beautiful hand painted brooches, hatpins and buttons are reflected on this ornate plateau mirror.

Limoges brooches, buttons, and boxes are sometimes categorized as specialty items or miniatures. There are many resources for the collector of Limoges boxes but overlooked are the Limoges brooches and buttons, hatpins and stick pins. These wonderful, tiny, exquisite extensions of Limoges art can be worn near to your heart on a daily basis as easily as you wear any other form of jewelry accessory.

During Queen Victoria's reign in England from 1837-1901 (with 1850-1900 being called the Victorian era) Limoges porcelain production in France was at its peak. Thanks to Queen Victoria, sentimentality sometimes superseded usefulness and there was great opulence in Europe and America. Combine the Victorians' love of art with one of their favorite pastimes, china painting, as well as the fad of the day for brooches and pins. Add their lust and romance with roses, along with their desire to emulate royalty, and one has the ingredients for some of the most elaborate and detailed pieces of tiny functional Limoges art. Queen Louise, Joan of Arch, Madame Pompadour, Raphael's Cherub, Josephine, Marie Antoinette, and George and Martha Washington were a few of the famous individuals painted on these brooches. In addition, china painters immortalized their female loved ones, and some of the most exquisite, well painted brooches and buttons are therefore hand painted with the homeliest of women. Beauty is in the eye of the beholder and to a relative this piece would be priceless.

The Victorian era was a time of great change and enlightenment, bringing with it the Machine Age, die stamping, and the invention of the pin-making machine. This simple machine made the attachments and devices for securing clothing and jewelry followed by more elaborate types of findings, clasps, and backings. This allowed for more detail and ornamentation and brooches became one of the decorative fashions of the era.

Due to the lack of modern laundry conveniences, collars, cuffs, waistbands, frills, and so on were detachable and kept in place by lace pins, safety pins, and bar pins. Tiny in size, one quarter of an inch to one inch, they could have been mistaken for baby or children's pins. Cuff pins were sold in pairs and waistband pins or "beauty pins" were worn in place of studs on the front of the waistband or on blouses and were sold in sets of three or four. Most featured intricate flowers in breathtaking detail, either hand painted, enameled, or transferred onto the porcelain. Tiny violets and forget-me-nots were among the favorites, although roses have always been ethereal. It is very rare to find a complete set today.

By the early 1900s, china painting was nearly a million dollar industry. Due to the popularity of such painting in the United States, Limoges and many other porcelain factories imported blanks by the thousands. The United States had over twenty-five thousand china painters, most of them woman. They painted all types of pieces, including jewelry such as brooches and accessories such as buttons, belt buckles, watch fobs. The blanks for many utilitarian accessories and brooches in a variety of shapes could be found in one of the china catalogs from the 1910s to the 1930s.

If your brooch, button, or accessory does not have a backstamp from one of the Limoges factories it will be difficult to determine if the brooch was hand painted on a piece of Limoges porcelain or on a piece that was exported from Germany or Austria. During the late nineteenth century and well into the twentieth century, the factories in Limoges were decorating brooches, earrings, and buttons in *décalcomanie*, the French term for transfer, specifically for export to the American market. These pieces are very common and easily identified because most are marked on the back "Made in France" or "Limoges France." Some are encased in gold, sterling silver, or gold and silver colored pot metal braided around the brooch. The metal may have a copper alloy so you may have some rust or a green corrosion showing. The clasp or finding on the back is a casted factory made clasp with a catch. You may run across a piece like this at a garage sale, flea market, or lower end antique shop and although not considered a piece of art it is still a wonderful collectible.

By examining the style of painting on your piece, you may be able to determine if it was decorated in France, by a European artist, or in the United States, by an American china painter. European decorated pieces are decorated in a quintessential impressionistic style, painted with superb cherubs, brilliantly colored and photo-realistic floral patterns, landscapes, wildlife, and Oriental motifs. American painted porcelain is distinct and was greatly influenced by the movements and fashion trends of a period. A particular period in history has a direct correlation with the painting style, composition, pattern, design, subject matter, motif, type of flower, color, amount of gold, and finish used (iridescent, luster, shiny or matte). Artistic inspiration came from natural sources but it is rare to find American porcelains decorated with landscapes, wilflife, or Oriental patterns. Naturalistic florals and fruits were the favorite subjects of the time in America, and artistic style and design was as unique as the thousands of individual American artists.

Collectors today can begin a fabulous collection of Limoges jewelry, including brooches, pins, buttons, and studs. The prices are reasonable and a constitute a fraction of the price for a larger piece of Limoges. The items are appealing, can be worn like any accessory, fit easily into a loved Limoges box, or make a tiny art vignette on a tabletop. Prices vary and are based on the uniqueness of shape and subject matter, detail and beauty of the painting, amount of gilt, and overall condition.

Brooches

Earrings, hand painted in a realistic style, are almost 1" diameter. Pair $50-$75.

Large, 3.2" brooch encased in solid 14kt gold can also be used as a pendant. $595-$795.

Earrings, hand painted with Joan of Arc, are encased in sterling silver and most likely hand painted by a European artist. Limoges France Mark 2, ca. after 1891. Pair $175-$275.

Oval, 2" brooch with "Mother" hand painted in gold. Marked "MADE IN Limoges FRANCE." $45-$50.

Ladies watch fob, 4.75" long, with "France" printed on the fob. $125-$150.

Elongated diamond shaped brooch, 1.75" wide, is an unusual shape. $40-$50.

Hand painted enamel belt buckle, 2.75" diameter, used with fabric sash belts, ca. 1900s. $250-$300.

Heart shaped brooch, 1.75 x 2". The heart was a popular romantic symbol from the Victorian era into the 1920s and is still among the most popular shapes. $75-$125.

Moon or crescent shaped brooch, 2" wide, is one of the oldest known shapes in jewelry design. $45-$75.

Rectangular 2.75" bar pin, is beautifully hand painted with exquisite violets and touches of gold. Usually used to hold collar ends together. $100-$125.

Rectangular 3" bar pin, an unusually long brooch of this style. Detailed dark red roses with tiny leaves are in perfect condition. $150-$175.

Tiny rectangular bar pin, not even 1" long, most likely a lace or cuff pin. $30-$40.

Diamond shaped, 1.5" brooch with raised enamel and portrait of Queen Louise. Exquisite detail of a prominent European figure most likely painted by a European artist. $175-$225.

Oval rose brooch, 1.5" x 2", also part of the set. This brooch would have been used at the bottom point of V-necked collars. $100-$125.

Oval rose brooch, 1.75" x 2.5", is part of a three piece set and decorated with beautiful dark roses. This brooch would have been used as the sash or belt buckle. $125-$150.

Unusually long bar pin, almost 3", used as a collar or scarf pin. $75-$80.

Round brooch, 1.25" diameter, is the last in the set. This brooch would have been used at the base of the collar. $75-$100.

Oval, 3" belt buckle brooch. Due to the large size and popularity of hand painted rose jewelry, pieces of this size run from $125-$250, depending on condition.

Oval, 3.2" belt buckle or sash brooch is painted with stunning multi-colored roses. $125-$150.

Oval, 2.75" brooch, with light roses hand painted in fine detail. $125-$150.

Oval, 3.2" and encased in solid gold, is very desirable and popular worn as a brooch. $250-$350.

Oval, 2.8" belt buckle or sash brooch is painted with tiny roses in painstaking detail. $125-$150.

Very large oval collar or sash brooch, 3" diameter. This brooch is stunning—with shading technique perfected and roses of exquisite detail—and is in high demand today by jewelry connoisseurs and hand-painting enthusiasts. $250-$350.

Round, 2.5" diameter brooch with heavy burnished gold and raised paste scrolls emulating the French style in vogue during the 1880s. $75-$90.

Oval, 3" brooch with exquisite detail and realism has gilt embellishment with raised gold dots on the edge. $125-$175.

Round, 2.25" diameter brooch with a touch of Art Deco geometric pattern at the very bottom. $50-$75.00

Oval, 2.25" brooch with pale pink roses and shaded green leaves. $125-$175.

Round, 3" diameter brooch with gold border and roses painted in more of a Monét style. $100-$125.

Oval, 1.25 x 1.75 brooch encased with braided gold. Back is marked "Made in France," ca. 1935. $100-$125.

Oval, 3" brooch with pale roses in Colonial Revival style, ca. 1900-1920. $100-$125.

Oval 2.5" brooch encased in gold braided pot metal. Back is marked "Limoges," ca. 1920-1930s. $100-$125.

Large oval 3" brooch with gold gilt edges that are outlined in black in more of the Art Deco style, ca. 1915-1930s. $125-150.

Oval, 3" brooch with burnished gold border and raised gold paste. $100-$125.

Large oval 3" brooch with heavy gold and lifelike roses. $100-$125.

Victorian rose brooch, 1.5", has heavy gold in perfect condition. $50-$75.

The poinsettia hand painted on this 1.5" x 2" brooch is not as common as other flowers. $50-$75.

Lovely oval brooch, 2" diameter, has beautiful shading and would be from the Aesthetic Movement, ca. 1875-1890. $100-$125.

Large 2" brooch with incredible detail on the branches and leaves. $125-$150.

Oval, 1.5" x 2" brooch with yellow roses. $50-$75.

Oval, 1.75" brooch has thick scrolled gold paste on the edge employing the French Style, ca. 1880s-1890s. $100-$125.

Small brooch less than .5" diameter was used as a lace or cuff pin. $25-$30.

Tiny round brooch depicting the solar system, a common theme and subject matter during the Victorian era, 1850-1900. Brooch, ca. 1900. $60-$70.

Tiny round brooch with less detail. $20-$40.

Large round brooch, 3.25" diameter, is painted in a naturalistic style with delicate detail. $225-$300.

Huge 3" oval brooch is a perfect example from the Aesthetic Movement, ca 1875-1890. $250-$300.

Tiny round brooch, less than .5" diameter, with violets painted in exquisite detail. $50-$75.

Large, lovely 3" brooch with less detail. $100-$125.

Oval, 2.5" brooch is another fine example from the Aesthetic Movement. $175-$200.

Oval, 2.5" brooch with French Style gilded rococo embellishment and fine hand painted flowers. $200-$225.

Oval, 3" brooch with hand painted forget-me-nots signifying true love. $75-$100.

Rare pendant, 1.25" diameter, with original gold plate over base metal back. $75-$100.

Oval, 2.5" brooch with detailed flowers and shading. $175-$200.

Large, 3.5" oval brooch, can be used as a pendant, has a portrait of Queen Louise in exquisite hand painted detail. Actual pearls have been used for her necklace and the piece is encased by sterling silver. $575-$775.

Large, 3.5" oval brooch, with fabulous colors and an unusual subject matter make this brooch of Martha Washington very desirable. Bezel-mounted in 14kt gold filled braid. $575-$775.

Oval, 2" enameled brooch encased in rococo style sterling silver frame. Hand painted, in beautiful detail, is a maiden holding a garland of roses. $575-$775.

Oval, 2" brooch has George Washington painted in detail with raised white enamel. $250-$275.

Oval, 2.5" brooch has painting of Raphael's Cherub in bezel-mounted frame with ornate detail edge. $375-$575.

Oval, 2" brooch with scrolled embellishment of gold gilt around the edge fading into the fancy gold bezel setting. Exquisite hand painting with raised enamel. $250-$275.

Oval, 1.75" brooch with religious subject, mounted in bezel set frame. $75-$125.

Oval, 2.5" brooch of the finest quality set in 14kt gold. $575-$775.

Desirable 2.25" cherub brooch has base metal back and was decorated using a partial transfer or *mixtion* process. $150-$175.

Oval, 2.5" brooch with ""Made in Limoges France" printed on the back is done completely in transfer. $100-$125.

Heart shaped, 2.5" brooch set in 14kt gold. Back has "Limoges France" and front has an illegible artist's signature. $575-$775.

Oval, 2" brooch with "Made in Limoges France" printed on the back. $125-$150.

Oval, 2.2" brooch with unidentified woman in hat. $150-$225.

Oval brooch of woman with plumed hat. $150-$225.

Small round portrait brooch with scrolled gold gilt on edges. $125-$145.

Oval brooch of woman with flapper style headdress. $150-$225.

Large, 2" oval brooch of a beautiful hand painted woman. The detail is exquisite and includes a beauty mark on the woman's cheek. $225-$250.

Oval brooch without metal back, stamped "Made in France." This piece is a mixture of transfer and hand painting. $75-$125.

Oval, 1.5" brooch with a portrait of an unknown woman. $125-$150.

Oval, 1.5" brooch encased in beveled frame with open back. "Made in France" printed in green on the back. $125-$150.

Oval, 1.75" brooch of European royalty is partial transfer. $125-$150.

Large 2" oval brooch, portrait of an unknown woman in a large plume hat. $125-$150.

Exquisite brooch, .75" diameter, enameled and set in 18kt gold. $175-$225.

Oval, 1.75" brooch of European royalty. Raised gold scrolled edging and enameled beads are part of the fine hand painted details. $225-$250.

Stick and Hatpins

Top of hatpin, 1" square, is a transfer of a woman and has been embellished with hand painted raised gilt ornamentation. $195-$225.

A tiny hand painted medallion is on the end of this 3.2" long stick pin used to hold ties and scarves. $50-$75.

Top of hatpin, 1.1" square, is a decal or transfer. $195-$225.

This top of a 9.2" long hatpin is a transfer of a woman. $195-$225.

Very desirable hatpin, 9" long, with George and Martha Washington. The set includes matching buttons using the transfer method of decoration. Set $195-$225.

Top of hatpin, 1.5" diameter, is transfer of a woman. $195-$225.

Buttons

Unusual, 1" square button with gold gilt and raised enamel dots of blue. $50-$75.

Buttons were a common form of porcelain hand painted by American china painters. These functional pieces of art are very inexpensive and make a great collection.

Button, .75" diameter, initials "AK" hand painted on the back. $25.

Button, .6" diameter. $25.

Pair of buttons. $25-$50.

Large button, 1.5" diameter, is part of a set. $50-$75.

Set of four matching buttons. Set $50-$75.

Pair of buttons. $25-$50.

Pair of buttons. $25-$50.

Unique set of four square matching buttons in two different sizes. Set $50-$75.

Large 2.5" brooch and pair of matching buttons, 1" diameter. Rare set $150-$250.

Large 1.2" button with violets. $35-$50.

Large 2.5" brooch and pair of matching buttons. All have raised gold dots and the brooch is also decorated with enameled dots of blue paint. Rare set $150-$250.

Set of buttons with raised enamel dots. Pair $25-$50.

Pair of buttons with forget-me-nots. Pair $25-$50.

Exquisite pair of buttons. Pair $25-$50.

Unique set of four hand painted buttons with different ladies painted on each. Embellished with scrolled and raised gold paste and done in fine detail, a set like this is very desirable for both the button and porcelain collector. Set $195-$225.

Three buttons, each with a different woman, are done in the transfer method. Although beautiful, they cannot compare with the hand painted set on the previous page. Set $75-$125.

Part IV

Researching Your Limoges

Identification Marks

Trying to identify a piece of Limoges porcelain can be as simple as turning the piece over and determining if the mark on the back is one of the approximately four hundred factory marks. This factory identification mark is called the **underglaze factory mark, the white ware mark, or the backstamp** and is usually green or black in color. Many of the factory marks were symbols, letters, or marks that were impressed, stamped, stenciled, or printed on the back of the piece under the glaze.

Identification is *not* as simple as the back stating "Limoges" or "Made in France," as many of the marks do not include the words France or Limoges. Due to the McKinley Tariff Act, after 1891 it was mandatory that all pieces imported to the United States be marked "France." After 1914, it was also mandatory for all pieces to state "Made in." However, most Limoges factories did not adhere to that requirement until after 1945, especially if their backstamp included the word Limoges or France.

It is difficult to identify and date one of the many unmarked pieces. Keep in mind that pieces normally not marked were pieces belonging to sets such as dinnerware and dresser sets, early snuff boxes, and pieces produced during the French Revolution. Becoming familiar with the various Limoges blanks and remembering that this type of hard paste porcelain does not craze will help you determine if it is Limoges.

Trying to determine if your piece was decorated in the factory is easy if you have a double backstamp, i.e., two marks on the back: the factory identification mark and the decorating mark. The decorating mark is also known as the **overglaze decorating mark**, as this mark is over the glaze. Although there is always the exception, most decorating marks come in a color other than green, such as red, blue, or purple.

If a piece of Limoges porcelain was hand painted in the factory, it would be easy to identify this if it simply stated "hand painted" or if a factory listed artist signed the piece on the front. Without the overglaze decorating mark or a listed French artist signature, however, confusion is easy and precise dating of a piece is harder. Limoges collectors may be able to identify pieces that were professionally factory decorated by associating a certain style of painting with a particular artist. For example, "Luc" is associated with painting game plates and plaques, portrait plaques, and figural decoration; "Dubois" with scenic plaques depicting animals, fish, and people along with game plates and platters; "Duval" with plaques, chargers, and plates having bird, fish, animals and scenic decorations; "Rene" with chargers and plates of game birds and animal decorations; and "Bronssillon" with vases, chargers, plaques, and plates painted with dark dramatic florals. In addition, the artists responsible for most factory painted pieces were directed to paint the pieces following a specific example—as a result, the decorations will appear to be very precise.

An underglaze factory mark, sometimes called the white ware mark or backstamp. This mark identifies the factory that produced the porcelain and is usually green or black in color. You cannot feel this mark when you run your finger across it, as it is "under the glaze."

Two distinct markings: the factory mark and the overglaze decorating mark. The overglaze decorating mark identifies the factory that decorated the porcelain. Shown is a decorating mark for the George Borgfeldt (Coronet) importing company. This mark is in green, but most decorating marks are usually in a color other than green such as red, blue, or purple. You can feel this mark when you run your finger across it, as it is "over the glaze."

A very rare William Guérin overglaze decorating mark in red.

A factory mark stating "Hand painted." Only some factory hand painted pieces have this mark.

As noted earlier, some of the most desired Limoges pieces are those that are factory decorated and signed by a particular artist. The following signatures are more predominant than others: Asselineau, Bronssillon, Dubois, Duval, Leroy, Luc, Magne, Max, Murville, Rene, and Rory. Some signatures command more in price, such as a Wagner signature on any piece of porcelain.

From the late nineteenth century to the early 1930s, Limoges pieces were imported blank to the United States and then decorated at one of the professional American decorating studios: The Art China Decorating Company, The Artistic Hand Painting Company, Jul. H. Brauer, Claremore Art Studio, Pairpoint, New Bedford, Massachusetts, Picard, Chicago, Stouffer, Chicago and White's Art Company, Chicago. These studios identified themselves with an overglaze decorating mark on the bottom of the piece of porcelain, along with the artist's signature somewhere on the piece.

There were also many smaller American decorating studios, such as The M. A. Bradford Studio and the New England China Painting Shop, both located in Boston, Massachusetts. These studios held classes for amateur American artists, teaching them the fine art of china painting. These smaller studios did not have an overglaze decorating mark but would paint their name on the bottom of the piece.

After learning the art of china painting, amateur artists could purchase blank pieces of Limoges porcelain that were imported to the United States and sold at fine department stores and studios. American amateur artists are responsible for most of the hand painted Limoges porcelain on the market today. On the bottom of these pieces will be the underglaze factory mark and then some place on the piece may be the artist's signature or initials and a date. Accurate family records are unavailable and it is difficult to identify exactly who these individuals were. A beautiful piece of Limoges, hand painted by a family member and passed down through generations, may reach the retail market without any information about the artist. Sad, except for the fact that a piece of Limoges hand painted by an American amateur artist is sometimes more desired by collectors than a piece decorated in the Limoges factories. And, although the exact history of the artist may be unknown, the price it commands may be high and the piece finds a sacred place in a private collection or home.

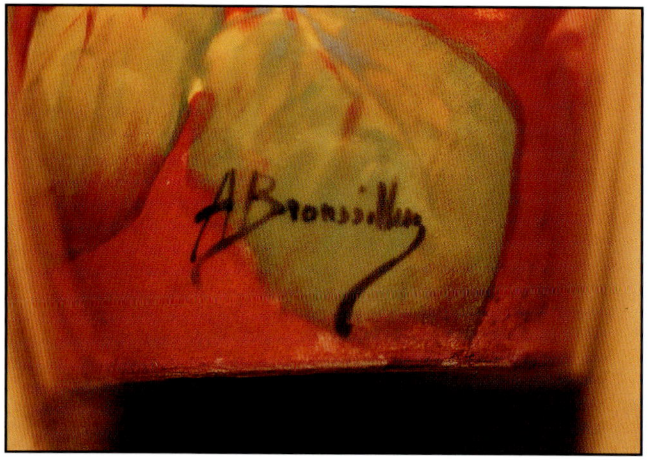

Left: The French listed artist's signature "A. Bronssillon" on the front of a piece.

Right: Sample of the Picard overglaze decorating mark, also common in gold. Picard was one of the American decorating studios.

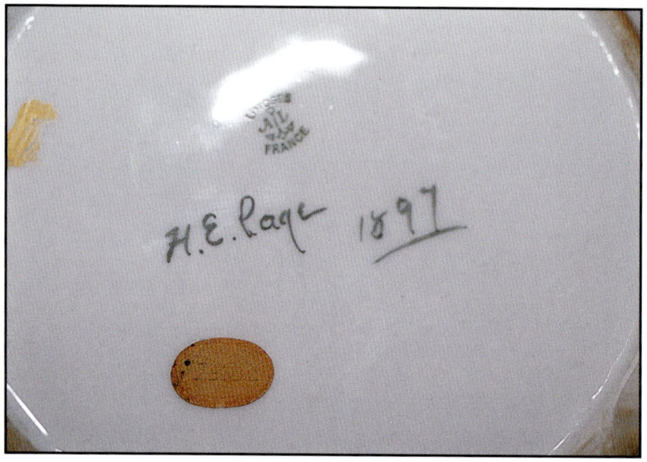

Left: Sample of the White's Art Company overglaze decorating mark. This company was another of the American decorating studios.

Right: Sample of an amateur artist's signature with date. The signature and date are on the bottom of the piece and over the glaze. In addition, this piece has the old import label, which is illegible.

Left and right: Sample of overglaze decorating marks from two small American decorating studios in Boston.

As discussed in an earlier section, there may be three marks on a piece of Limoges: the underglaze factory identification mark, the overglaze decorating mark, and the **export or import mark**. The export mark is from the exporter in France. The import marks are usually easy to identify as they specifically state the retail department or jewelry store that ordered the piece or set to sell to the American public. Some confusion is possible because the import mark was sometimes used in place of the factory decorating mark, but such pieces were decorated in one of the factories in Limoges. Several retail importers, whose names you may see on the back of a piece of Limoges, are Bailey, Banks and Biddle, Philadelphia; Tiffany's, New York; and Wanamaker's, Washington, D.C.

An import mark for Wanamaker's department store in Philadelphia, which imported many pieces of Limoges to sell to the American market. This mark is over the glaze and can be felt by running your finger across the mark. Also shown is the overglaze decorating mark in red.

Sample of an import mark specifically for the Haviland & Co., Limoges factory. Sometimes pieces and complete sets were made for a specific family.

Common Porcelain Factory and Decorating Marks

Organized in alphabetical order, this section provides actual photographs or artist renditions of the most common factory marks expressed in letters, marks, or symbols. Identified as the underglaze factory mark or overglaze decorating mark, all marks are accompanied by their actual color and the dates the factory was in operation. In order to eliminate confusion, the numbering of these marks is consistent with the published works by Mary Frank Gaston.

Charles J. Ahrenfeldt Marks, 1859 to 1969

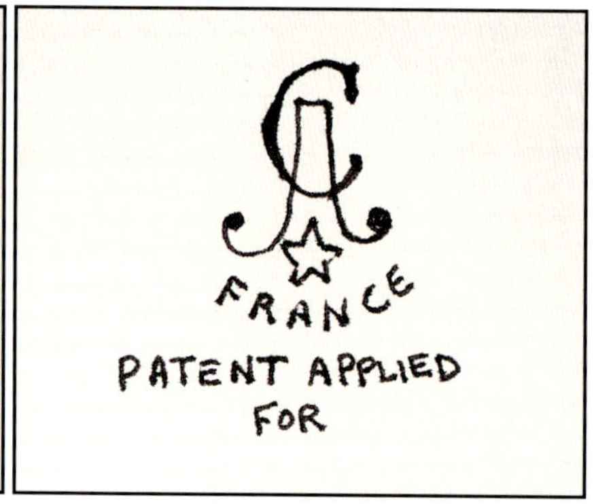

Left to right:
Ahrenfeldt, overglaze decorating mark in red. 1884-1893.

Ahrenfeldt, Mark 1 in blue Overglaze decorating mark. After 1893.

Ahrenfeldt, Mark 2 in green. Underglaze factory mark. 1894-1930s.

Ahrenfeldt, Mark 3 in green. Underglaze factory mark. 1894-1930s.

Left to right:
Ahrenfeldt, Mark 4 in green. Underglaze factory mark. 1894-1930s.

Ahrenfeldt, Mark 5 in green. Underglaze factory mark. 1894-1930s.

Ahrenfeldt, Mark 6 in green. Underglaze factory mark. 1894-1930s.

Ahrenfeldt, Mark 7 in green. Overglaze decorating mark. 1894-1930s.

Ahrenfeldt, Mark 8a in green, red, or gold. Overglaze decorating mark. 1894-1930s.

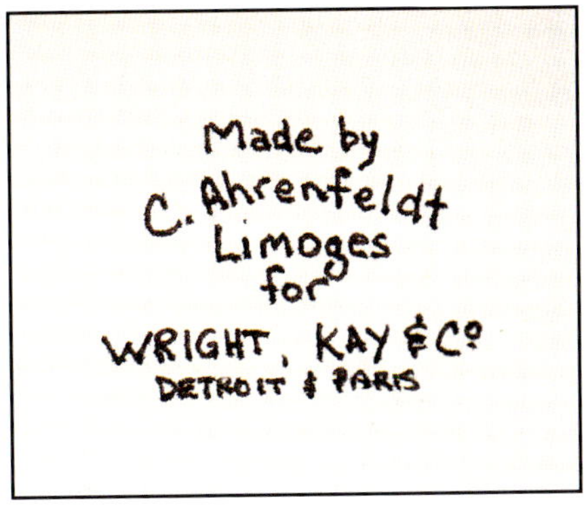

Ahrenfeldt, Mark 8b in green. Overglaze decorating mark. 1894-1930s.

Ahrenfeldt, Mark 8b, another example of an overglaze decorating mark. 1894-1930s.

Ahrenfeldt, Mark 9 in blue. Overglaze decorating mark. After World War II until 1969.

Bawo & Dotter Marks (Elite Works), 1860s to 1932

Top row, left to right:
Bawo & Dotter, Mark 1 in green. Overglaze decorating mark. 1870s-1880s.
Bawo & Dotter, Mark 2 in green. Overglaze decorating mark. 1870s-1880s.
Bawo & Dotter, Mark 2a in red. Overglaze decorating mark. 1870s-1880s.
Bawo & Dotter, Mark 3 in red or green. Overglaze decorating mark. 1880s.

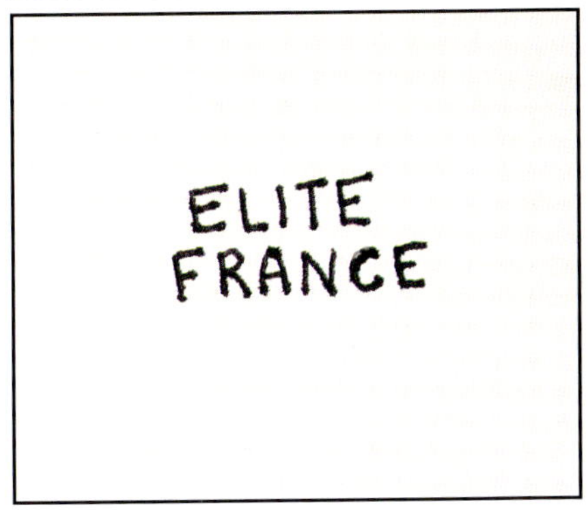

Bottom row, left to right:
Bawo & Dotter, Mark 4 in green. Underglaze factory mark. 1896-1900.
Bawo & Dotter, Mark 5 in green. Underglaze factory mark. After 1900.
Bawo & Dotter, Mark 6 in red. Overglaze decorating mark. 1880s-1891.
Bawo & Dotter, Mark 7. Underglaze factory mark in green, overglaze decorating mark in red. 1896-1900.

Bawo & Dotter, Mark 8 in red. Overglaze decorating mark. 1896-1900.

Bawo & Dotter, Mark 9 in red. Overglaze decorating mark. 1900-1914.

Bawo & Dotter, Mark 10 in red. Overglaze decorating mark. 1900-1914.

Bawo & Dotter, Mark 11 in red. Overglaze decorating mark. 1920-1932.

Bawo & Dotter, Mark 12 in black and brown. Overglaze decorating mark. After 1920.

Bernardaud & Co. (B&Co.), 1900 to present

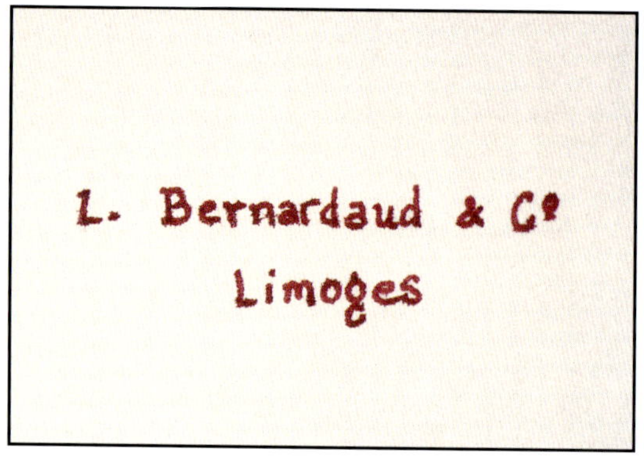

Left to right:
Bernardaud & Co., Mark 1 in green. Underglaze factory mark. 1900-1914.

Bernardaud & Co., Mark 2 in green. Underglaze factory mark. 1914-1930s and after.

Bernardaud & Co., Mark 3 in red. Overglaze decorating mark. 1900-1930s and after.

Blakeman & Henderson (B. & H.), 1900s

Left to right:
Blakeman & Henderson, Mark 1 in green, gray, or red. Circle, overglaze decorating mark. 1890s-1900s.

Blakeman & Henderson, Mark 2 in green. Script mark, overglaze decorating mark. Early 1900s.

Blakeman & Henderson, Mark 3 in green. Overglaze decorating mark with script mark and circle mark in green. Early 1900s.

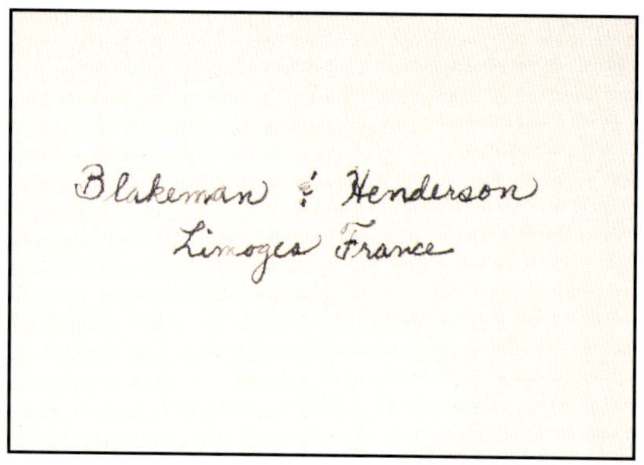

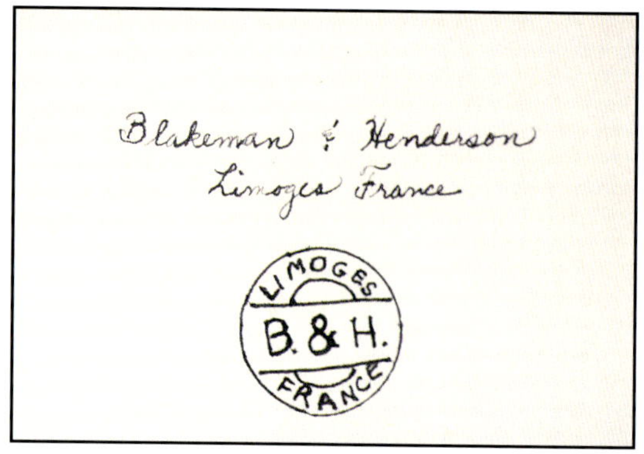

George Borgfeldt (Coronet), 1881 to 1976, U.S. Importer

Borgfeldt, George (Coronet), Mark 1 in green or blue. Overglaze decorating mark. 1906-1920.

Borgfeldt, George (Coronet), Mark 2 in green. Overglaze decorating mark. After 1920.

Coiffe Marks, 1870s to mid 1920s

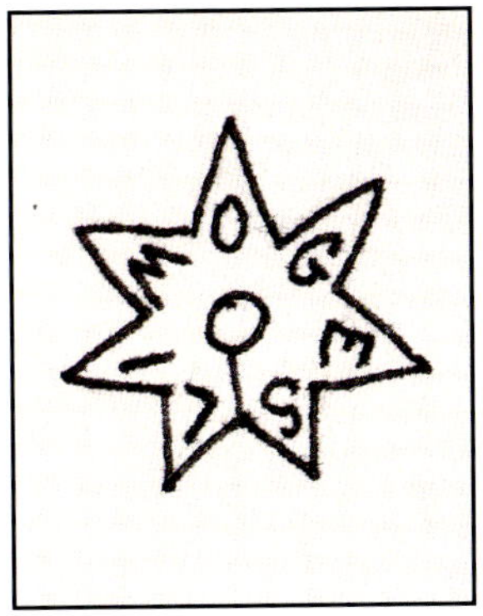

Coiffe, Mark 1 in green. Underglaze factory mark. Before 1890.

Coiffe, Mark 2 in green. Underglaze factory mark. After 1891-1914.

Coiffe, Mark 3 in green. Underglaze factory mark. After 1891-1914.

Coiffe, Mark 4 in green. Underglaze factory mark. 1914-1920s.

Délinières, R. (D&Co.), 1860 to 1900

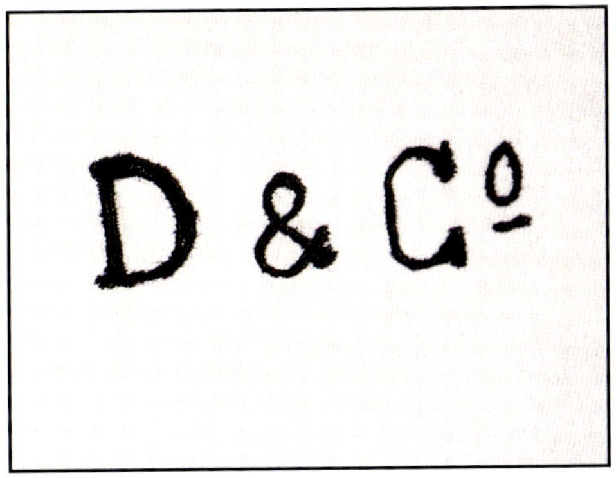

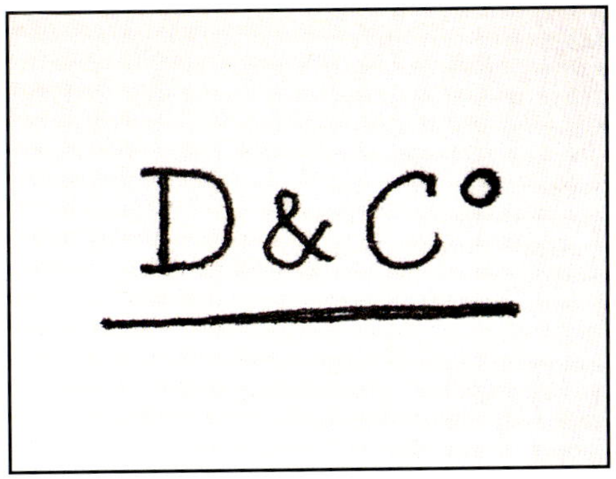

Left to right:
Délinières, R. (D&Co.), Mark 1 in green. Underglaze factory mark. 1870s.

Délinières, R. (D&Co.), Mark 2 in green. Underglaze factory mark. 1879-1893

Délinières, R. (D&Co.), Mark 3 in green. Underglaze factory mark. 1894-1900.

Délinières, R. (D&Co.), Mark 4 in red. Overglaze decorating mark. 1881-1893.

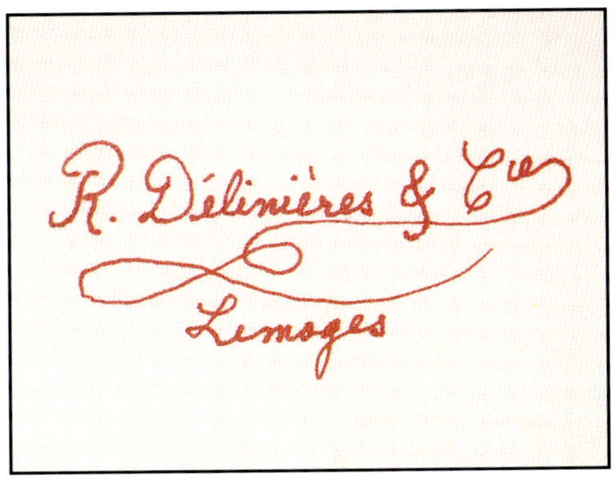

Left to right:
Délinières, R. (D&Co.), Mark 5 in red. Overglaze decorating mark in script form. 1894-1900.

Délinières, R. (D&Co.), Mark 6 in red. Overglaze decorating mark with importer.

Flambeau China Marks (L.D.B.& Co.), late 1890s to World War I

Flambeau China, Mark 1 in green. Underglaze factory mark. 1890s-1914.

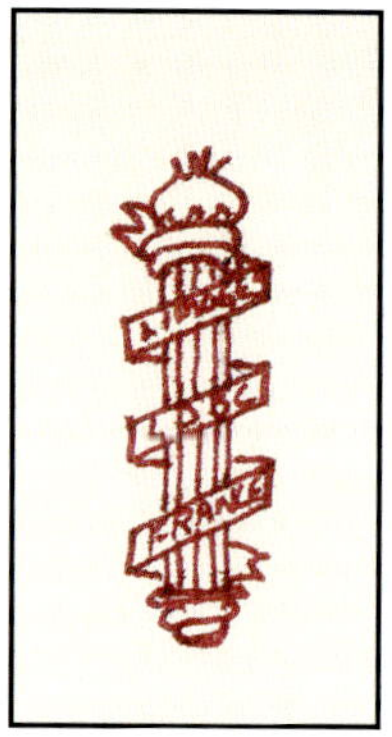

Flambeau China, Mark 2 in red. Overglaze decorating mark. 1890s, used prior to factory producing porcelain.

Flambeau China, Mark 3 in green, red, or blue. Overglaze decorating mark. 1890s-early 1900s.

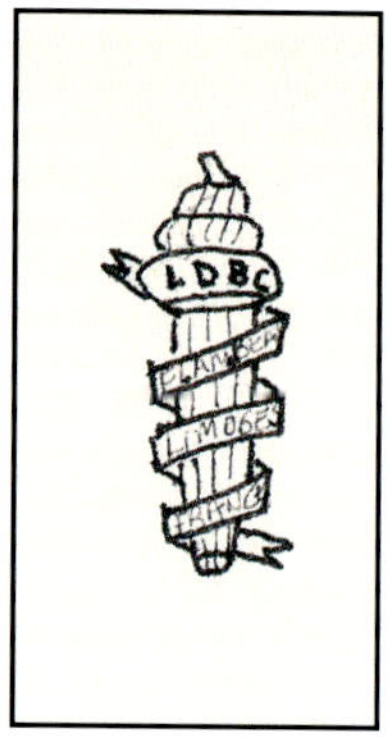

Flambeau China, Mark 4 in green. Overglaze decorating mark. 1890s-early 1900s.

Flambeau China, Mark 5 in green. Overglaze decorating mark. Before 1914 and after Marks 2, 3, and 4.

Flambeau China, Mark 6 in green. Overglaze decorating mark. Before 1914 and after Marks 2, 3, and 4.

Gérard, Dufraisseix and Abbot (GDA) Marks, 1900 to present

Gérard, Dufraisseix, and Abbot, Mark 1 in green. Underglaze factory mark. 1900-1941.

Gérard, Dufraisseix, and Abbot, Mark 2 in green. Underglaze factory mark. Early 1900s.

Gérard, Dufraisseix, and Abbot, Mark 3 in red. Overglaze decorating mark. 1900-1941.

Gérard, Dufraisseix, and Abbot, Mark 4 in red. Overglaze decorating mark. 1941 to present.

Gérard, Dufraisseix, and Morel Marks (GDM), 1881 to 1890

Gérard, Dufraisseix, and Morel, Mark 1 in green. Underglaze factory mark. 1882-1890.

Gérard, Dufraisseix, and Morel, Mark 2 in green. Underglaze factory mark. After 1891-1900.

Gérard, Dufraisseix, and Morel, Mark 3 in red, blue, gray, brown, or black. Overglaze decorating mark. 1882-1900.

Granger Marks, 1922-1938

Granger, Mark 1 in green. Underglaze factory mark. 1922-1938.

Granger, Mark 2 in green. Underglaze factory mark. 1922-1938.

Granger, Mark 3 in black and gold. Overglaze decorating mark. 1922-1938.

William Guérin Marks (W.G.&Co.), 1836 to 1932

Guérin, Mark 1 in green. Underglaze factory mark. 1870s.

Guérin, Mark 2 in green. Underglaze factory mark. 1891-1900.

Guérin, Mark 3 in green. Underglaze factory mark. 1900-1932.

Guérin, Mark 4 in red, blue, green, brown, or gold. Overglaze decorating mark. 1800s-1932.

Haviland Marks

HAVILAND & CIE. 1842-1931

BLANKS:

Mark A — HAVILAND — Incised on Tablet — 1853

Mark B — HAVILAND H&Co — Incised — 1865

Underglaze Green Marks

Mark C — H&Co — 1876-1879

Mark D — H&Co — 1876-1886

Mark E — H&Co — 1877

Mark F — H&Co L — 1876-1889

Mark G — H&Co DEPOSE — 1887

Mark H — H&Co L FRANCE — 1888-1896

Mark I — Haviland France — 1894-1931

DECORATOR MARKS:

Varied Colors Overglaze

Mark a — FABRIQUÉ PAR HAVILAND & Co POUR J.W. BOTELER & BRO. WASHINGTON — prior to 1876

Mark b — 1876-1878

Mark c — HAVILAND & Co Limoges — 1876-1878/1889-1931

Mark d — HAVILAND & Co — 1879-1883

Mark e — H&Co ELITE — 1878-1883

Mark f — H&Co SPECIAL — 1879-1889

Mark g — HAVILAND LIMOGES — 1879-1889

Mark h — Limoges Feu de Four — 1893-1931

Mark i — Décoré par HAVILAND & Co Limoges — 1905-1930 (America) 1926-1931 (France)

HAVILAND & Co. 1875-1885

Haviland Pottery and Stoneware

Mark V — H&Co L — 1875-1882

Mark W — HAVILAND & Co Limoges — 1875-1882

Mark X — H&Co — 1883-1885

Mark Y — H&Co L HAVILAND — 1883-1885

Haviland & Cie marks. *Courtesy of Haviland Collectors Internationale Foundation.*

FRANK HAVILAND 1910-1931

BLANKS:

Mark A1 — FRANK HAVILAND LIMOGES — 1910-1914

Mark A2 — Frank Haviland Limoges — 1914-1925

Mark A3 — FRANK HAVILAND LBS LIMOGES — 1925-1931

THÉODORE HAVILAND 1892-1967

BLANKS:

Colors Usually Green Underglaze

Mark J — 1892

Mark K — MONT MERY FRANCE — 1892

Mark L — Théo Haviland Limoges FRANCE — 1893

Mark M — T H — 1894-1957

Mark N — Blue — 1912

Mark O — 1920-1936

Mark P — THEODORE HAVILAND — 1936-1945

Mark Q — Haviland France — 1946-1962

Mark R — Haviland France Limoges — 1962

Mark S — THEODORE HAVILAND NEW YORK — Green or Black — 1936

Mark T — Theodore Haviland New York MADE IN AMERICA — Red or Black — 1937-1956

Mark U — HAVILAND U.S.A. — Red — 1957

DECORATOR MARKS:

Colors Green and/or Red Underglaze

Mark j — Red — probably 1892

Mark k — Porcelaine Mousseline Limoges FRANCE — 1894

Mark l — Porcelaine Mousseline T H Limoges FRANCE — 1894

Mark m — Porcelaine Theo. Haviland Limoges FRANCE — 1895

Mark n — Porcelaine Theo. Haviland Limoges FRANCE — 1895

Mark o — Théodore Haviland Limoges — 1897

Mark p — Théodore Haviland Limoges FRANCE — 1903

Mark q — Théodore Haviland Limoges FRANCE — 1903

Mark r — Théodore Haviland Limoges FRANCE — 1925

Mark s — HAVILAND LIMOGES — 1958

Mark t — Haviland — 1967

76

Frank and Theodore Haviland marks and dates. *Courtesy of Haviland Collectors Internationale Foundation.*

A. Klingenberg (AK)/Charles Dwenger (AKCD) Marks, 1880s to 1910

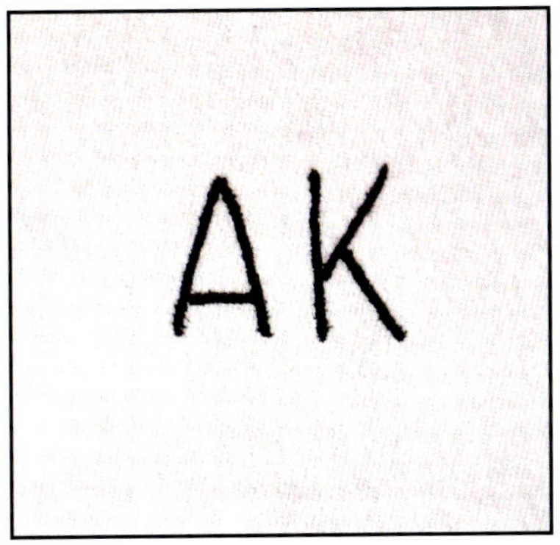

Left to right:
Klingenberg, Mark 1 in red. Overglaze decorating mark. Early 1880s.

Klingenberg, Mark 2 in red. Overglaze decorating mark. 1880s-1890s.

Klingenberg, Mark 3 in green. Impressed or underglaze factory mark. 1880s-1890.

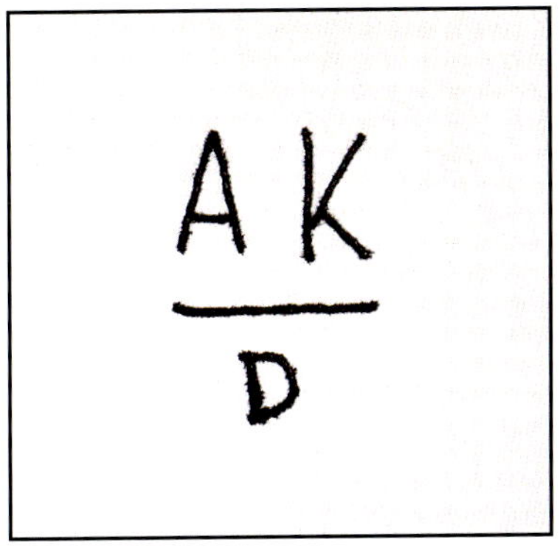

Left to right:
Klingenberg, Mark 4 in green. Underglaze factory mark. After 1891.

Klingenberg, Mark 5 in green. Underglaze factory mark. 1890s.

Klingenberg, Mark 6 in green. Underglaze factory mark. 1890s-1910, but after Mark 5.

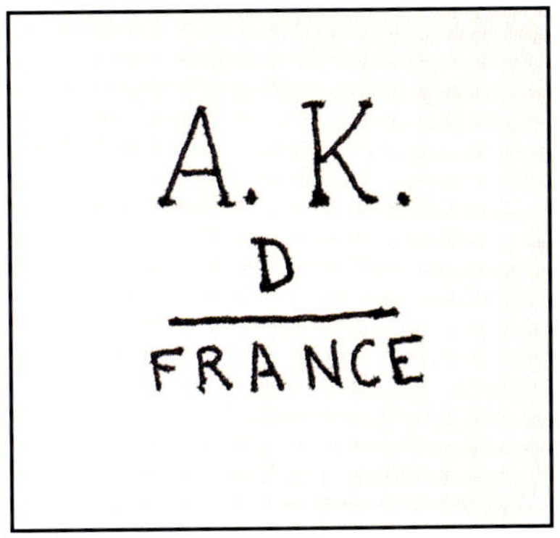

Left to right:
Klingenberg, Mark 7 in green. Underglaze factory mark. 1890s-1910.

Klingenberg, Mark 8 in green. Underglaze factory mark. 1890s-1910.

Klingenberg, Mark 9 in red. Overglaze decorating mark. 1900-1910.

A. Laternier Marks, 1857 to present

Top row, left to right:
Lanternier, Mark 1 in red. Overglaze decorating mark. 1890s.
Lanternier, Mark 2 in green. Underglaze factory mark. 1890s.
Center row, left to right:
Lanternier, Mark 3 in green. Underglaze factory mark. 1890s.
Lanternier, Mark 4 in green. Underglaze factory mark. 1891-1914.
Lanternier, Mark 5 in blue. Overglaze exporting or decorating mark. Before 1890.
Bottom row, left to right:
Lanternier, Mark 6 in red, brown, or blue. Overglaze decorating mark. 1891-1914.
Lanternier, Mark 7 in red and black. Overglaze decorating mark. After World War I.

La Porcelaine Limousine (PL) Marks, 1906 to 1938

Left to right:
La Porcelaine Limousine, Mark 1 in green. Underglaze factory mark. 1905-1930s.
La Porcelaine Limousine, Mark 2 in green. Underglaze factory mark. 1905-1930s.
La Porcelaine Limousine, Mark 3 in green. Underglaze factory mark. 1905-1930s.
La Porcelaine Limousine, Mark 4 in red. Overglaze decorating mark. 1905-1930s.

Lazeyras, Rosenfeld, and Lehman Marks (LR&L), 1920s

Left to right:
Lazeyras, Rosenfeld, and Lehman (LR&L), Mark 1 in red or blue. Overglaze decorating mark. 1920s.

Lazeyras, Rosenfeld, and Lehman, Mark 2 in red. Overglaze decorating mark. 1920s.

Lazeyras, Rosenfeld, and Lehman, Mark 3 in gray or green. Overglaze decorating mark. 1920s.

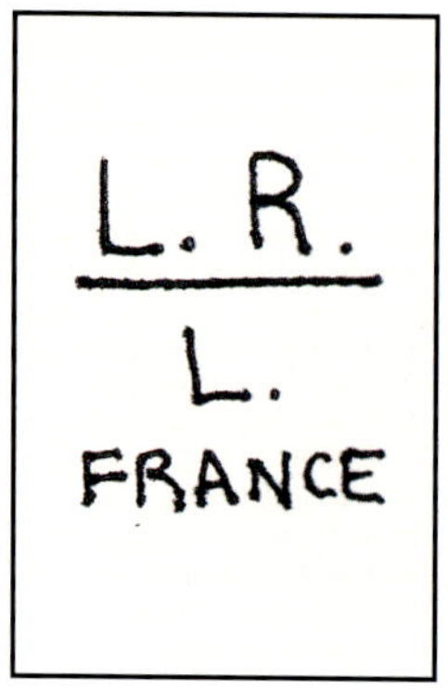

Left to right:
Lazeyras, Rosenfeld, and Lehman, Mark 4 in blue. Overglaze decorating mark. After 1922.

Lazeyras, Rosenfeld, and Lehman, Mark 5 in blue. Overglaze decorating mark. After 1922.

Legrand Mark, 1920s

Legrand, Mark in green. Underglaze factory mark. 1920s.

Limoges France Marks, 1891 and after

Limoges France, Mark 1 in green. Underglaze factory mark. After 1891.

Limoges France, Mark 2 in green. Underglaze factory mark. After 1891.

Limoges France, Mark 3 in green. Underglaze factory mark. After 1891.

Limoges France, Mark 4 in green. Underglaze factory mark. After 1891.

Limoges France, Mark 5 in green. Underglaze factory mark. After 1891.

Limoges France, Mark 6 in green. Underglaze factory mark. After 1891.

Limoges France, Mark 7 in green. Underglaze factory mark. After 1891.

Limoges France, Mark 8 in blue. Overglaze decorating or exporting mark. After 1891.

Limoges France, Mark 9 in gray. Overglaze decorating mark. After 1908.

Charles Martin Marks, 1880s to 1935

Martin, Mark 1 in green. Underglaze factory mark. After 1891.

Martin, Mark 2 in green. Underglaze factory mark. Early 1900s-1930s.

Martin, Mark 3 in blue or green. Overglaze decorating mark. Early 1900s-mid 1930s.

P.M. Mavaleix, 1908 to 1914

Mavaleix, Mark in green. Underglaze factory mark. 1908-1914.

Pairpoint Mark, 1880s to 1900

Pairpoint, mark in green. Overglaze decorating mark for American decorating factory. 1880s.

Paroutaud Freres, 1902 to 1916

Paroutaud Freres, Mark 1 in green. Underglaze factory mark. 1903-1917.

Paroutaud Freres, Mark 2 in green. Underglaze factory mark. 1903-1917.

Plainemaison, c. 1890s to c. 1910

Plainemaison, Mark 1 in green. Underglaze factory mark. 1890s-1910.

Jean Pouyat Marks (JP), 1832 to 1932

Top row, left to right: Pouyat, Jean, Mark 1 in green. Underglaze factory mark. 1850s-1875.
Pouyat, Jean, Mark 2 in red. Overglaze decorating mark. 1850s-1875.
Pouyat, Jean, Mark 3 in green. Underglaze factory mark. After 1876-1890.
Center row, left to right: Pouyat, Jean, Mark 4 in red. Overglaze decorating mark. 1876-1890.
Pouyat, Jean, Mark 5 in green. Underglaze factory mark. 1891-1932.
Pouyat, Jean, Mark 6 in red. Overglaze decorating mark. After 1890, used for a short time.
Bottom row, left to right: Pouyat, Jean, Mark 7 in red. Overglaze decorating mark. 1890s-1914.
Pouyat, Jean, Mark 8 in green. Overglaze decorating mark. 1914-1932.
Pouyat, Jean, Mark 9, in green and pink. Overglaze decorating mark. 1914-1932.

Martial Redon Marks (MR), 1882 to 1896

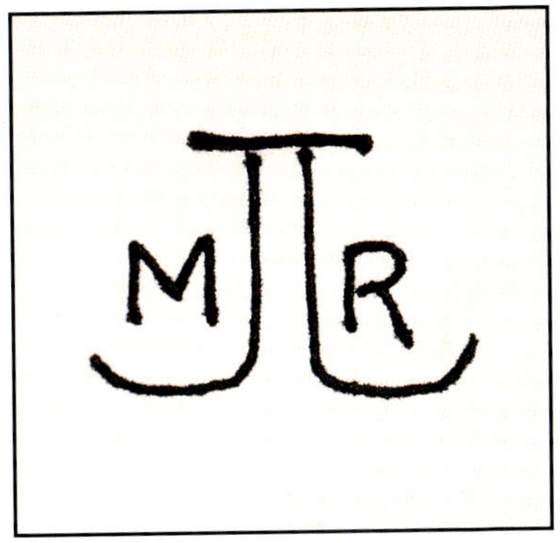

Redon, M., Mark 1 in green. Underglaze factory mark. 1882-1890.

Redon, M., Mark 2 in green. Underglaze factory mark. 1891-1896.

Redon, M., Mark 2a in green. Underglaze factory mark with the word "Limoges."

Redon, M., Mark 3 in red or blue. Overglaze decorating mark. 1882-1896.

Redon, M., Mark 4 in red. Overglaze decorating mark. 1882-1896.

Lewis Straus and Sons Marks (LS&S), 1890s to 1920s

Straus, Lewis and Sons mark in green, blue, red, or gray. Overglaze exporting mark. 1890s-1920.

Tressemann & Vogt Marks (T&V), early 1880s to 1907

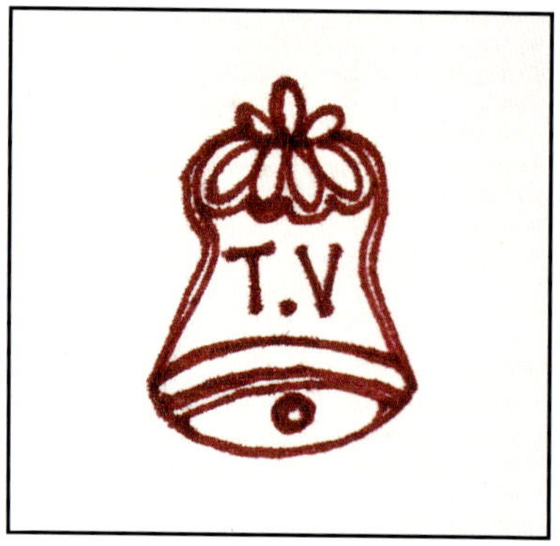

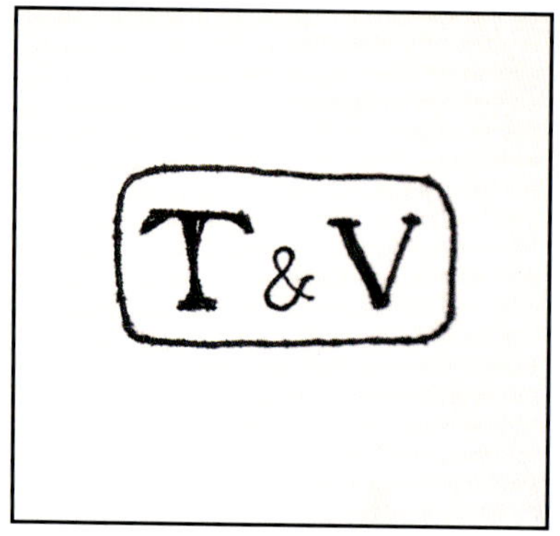

Left to right:
Tressemann & Vogt, Mark 1 in blue. Overglaze exporting mark. 1880s-1891.

Tressemann & Vogt, Mark 2 in purple, red, or gold. Overglaze decorating mark. Early 1880s.

Tressemannn & Vogt, Mark 3 in brown. Overglaze decorating mark. After 1891, very rare.

Tressemann & Vogt, Mark 4a, in green. Underglaze factory mark. Early 1890s.

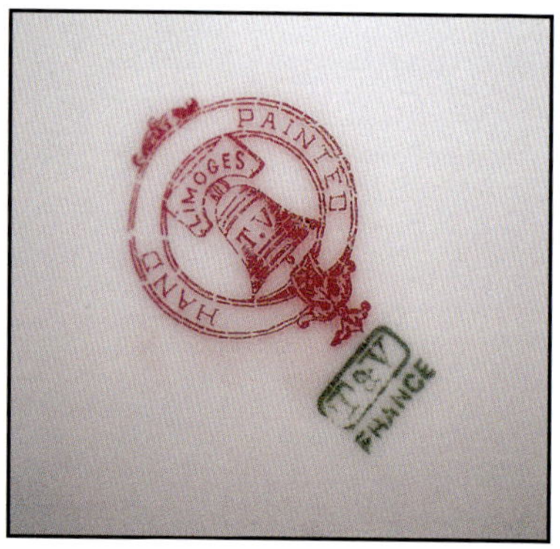

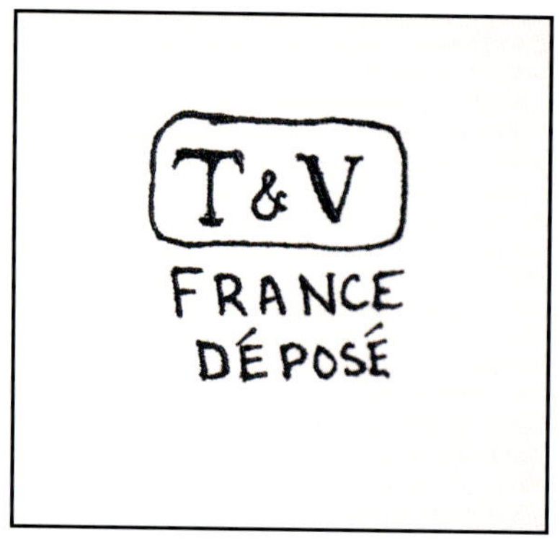

Left to right:
Tressemann & Vogt, Mark 4b, in green. Underglaze factory mark. 1892-1907 but before Mark 5a.

Tressemann & Vogt, Mark 5a in green. Underglaze factory mark. 1892-1907.

Tressemann & Vogt, Mark 5b in green. Underglaze factory mark. Found on items decorated with famous people or commemorative events.

Tressemann & Vogt, Mark 6 in green. Underglaze factory mark. 1892-1907, around 1900s.

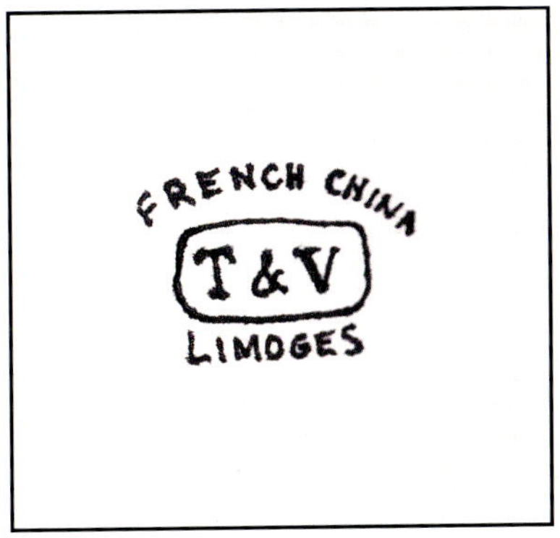

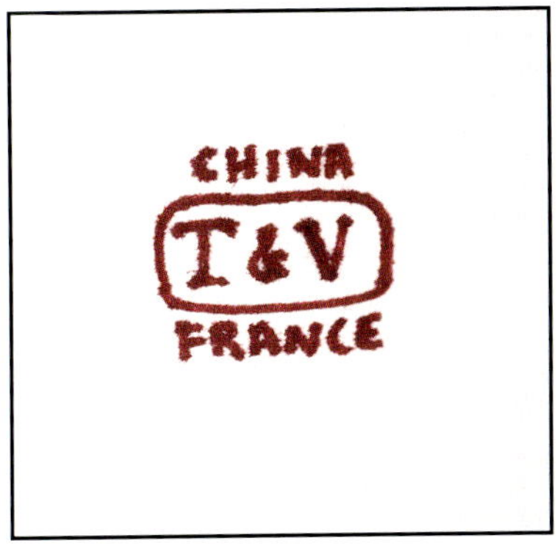

Top row, left to right:
Tressemann & Vogt, Mark 7 in green. Underglaze factory mark. 1892-1907, latter part of period.

Tressemann & Vogt, Mark 8 in green. Underglaze factory mark. 1907-1919.

Tressemann & Vogt, Mark 9 in purple. Overglaze decorating mark. 1892-1907, early part of period.

Tressemann & Vogt, Mark 10 in red or gold. Overglaze decorating mark. 1892-1907, about 1900.

Center row, left to right:
Tressemann & Vogt, Mark 11 in red, brown, or gold. Overglaze decorating mark. 1892-1907, latter part of period.

Tressemann & Vogt, Mark 12 in purple. Overglaze decorating mark. 1907-1919, very rare.

Tressemann & Vogt, Mark 13 in red. Overglaze decorating mark. 1907-1919, very rare.

Tressemann & Vogt, Mark 14 in green. Overglaze decorating mark. 1907-1919, very rare.

Bottom row, left to right:
Tressemann & Vogt, Mark 15 in purple. Overglaze decorating mark.

Tressemann & Vogt, Mark 16 in purple. Overglaze decorating mark. 1907-1919.

Tressemann & Vogt, Mark 16b, in purple. Overglaze decorating mark, like Mark 16 with addition of banner with "Hand Painted." 1907-1919.

Union Céramique Marks (UC), 1909 to 1938

Left to right:
Union Céramique, Mark 1 in green. Underglaze factory mark. 1909-1938.

Union Céramique, Mark 2 in red. Overglaze decorating mark. 1909-1938.

Wanamaker's Mark, 1900s

Wanamaker's mark in green. Overglaze importing mark. Early 1900s.

Vignaud Frères Marks, 1911 to 1970

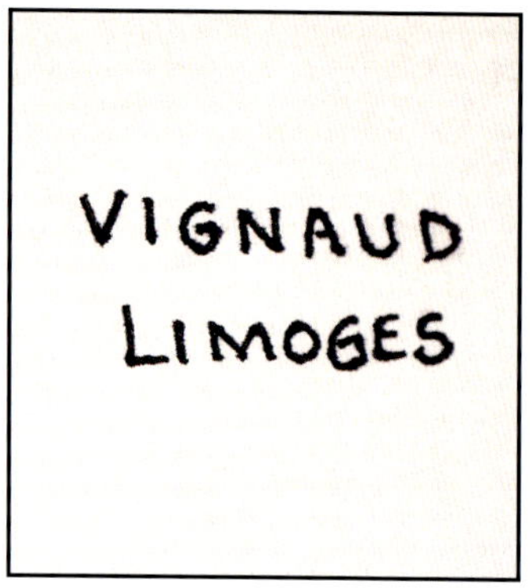

Vignaud Frères, Mark 1 in green. Underglaze factory mark. After 1911-1938.

Vignaud Frères, Mark 2 in green. Overglaze decorating mark. 1911-1938.

Vignaud Frères, Mark 3 in green. Underglaze factory mark. 1938 and after.

Bibliography

Albis, Jean d', and Celeste Romanet. *La Porcelaine de Limoges*. Paris: Sous le Vent, 1980.

Allon, Janet. *The Business of Bliss, How to Profit from Doing What You Love*. New York, New York: Hearst Books, 1999.

Baker, Lillian, *Baker's Encyclopedia of Hatpins & Hatpin Holders*. Atglen, Pennsylvania: Schiffer Publishing, Ltd., 1998.

Baker, Lillian. *100 Years of Collectible Jewelry*. Paducah, Kentucky: Collector Books, 1989.

Bell, Jeanenne. *Old Jewelry. Second Edition*. Florence, Alabama: Books Americana, Inc., 1985.

Cameron, Elisabeth. *Encyclopedia of Pottery and Porcelain: 1800-1960*. New York, New York: Facts on File Publications, 1986.

Celebrating 150 Years of Haviland China: 1842-1992. Haviland Collectors Internationale Foundation, 1992.

Chefetz, Sheila. *Antiques for the table*. New York: Penguin Books USA, Inc., 1993.

Ettinger, Roseann. *Popular Jewelry 1840-1940*. Atglen, Pennsylvania: Schiffer Publishing, Ltd., 1997.

Gaston, Mary Frank. *The Collector's Encyclopedia of Limoges Porcelain. Second Edition*. Paducah, Kentucky: Collector Books, 1994.

Gaston, Mary Frank. *The Collector's Encyclopedia of Limoges Porcelain. Third Edition*. Paducah, Kentucky: Collector Books, 2000.

Hynes, Angela. *The Pleasures of Afternoon Tea*. Los Angeles, California: HP Books, 1987.

Israel, Andrea. *Taking Tea*. New York, New York: Michael Friedman Publishing Group, Inc., 1988.

Kamm, Dorothy. *Antique Trader's Comprehensive Guide to American Painted Porcelain*. Norfolk, Virginia: Antique Trader Books, 2000.

Kamm, Dorothy. *American Painted Porcelain: Collector's Identification and Value Guide*. Paducah, Kentucky: Collector Books, 1997, values updated 1999.

Kamm, Dorothy. "American Painted Porcelain Jewelry: Miniature Masterpieces." *Antiques & Collecting Magazine*, Volume 105, Number 2 (April 2000); 32-37.

King, M. Dalton. *Special Teas*. Philadelphia, Pennsylvania: A Running Press/Kenan Book, 1992.

Kovel, Ralph M., and Terry H. Kovel. *Dictionary of Marks: Pottery and Porcelain*. New York: Crown Publishers, Inc., 1953 and 1972.

Kovel, Ralph, and Terry Kovel. *Kovels' New Dictionary of Marks*. New York: Crown Publishers, Inc., 1986.

Lehner, Lois. *Lehner's Encyclopedia of U.S. Marks on Pottery, Porcelain & Clay*. Paducah, Kentucky: Collector Books, 1988.

Manchester, Carole. *French Tea, The Pleasures of the Table*. New York: Hearst Books, 1993.

Pearon, Katherine. *Accent on Accessories*. Birmingham, Alabama: Oxmoor House, 1995.

Phillips, Phoebe. *The Collectors' Encyclopedia of ANTIQUES*. London England: Crown Publishing, 1978.

Revi, Albert Christian. *The Spinning Wheel's Complete Book of Antiques*. New York: Grosset & Dunlap, 1977.

Reed, Alan B. *Encyclopedia of Picard China*. Paducah, Kentucky: Collector Books, 1995.

Sandon, Henry. *Coffee Pots and Tea Pots for the Collector.* New York: Arco Publishing Co., Inc., 1974.

Stewart, Martha. *Living*. December 1994 and January 1995.

Strumpf, Faye. *Limoges Boxes, A Complete Guide*. Iola, Wisconsin: Krause Publications, 2000.

Travis, Nora. *Haviland China: The Age of Elegance*. Atglen, Pennsylvania: Schiffer Publishing, Ltd., 1997.

Waterbrook-Clyde, Keith and Thomas. *The Decorative Art of Limoges, Porcelain and Boxes*. Atglen, Pennsylvania: Schiffer Publishing, Ltd., 1999.

Wynter, Harriet. *An Introduction to European Porcelain*. New York: Thomas Y. Crowell Company, 1972.

Index

Index